MW01291973

Garth,
I am glad u
are teammates.
#I GOT you.
7/5/19

A BROTHER'S LOVE
A Memoir

BY
MATTHEW CUBBLER

Bloomington, IN Milton Keynes, UK

authorHOUSE

AuthorHouse™
1663 Liberty Drive, Suite 200
Bloomington, IN 47403
www.authorhouse.com
Phone: 1-800-839-8640

AuthorHouse™ UK Ltd.
500 Avebury Boulevard
Central Milton Keynes, MK9 2BE
www.authorhouse.co.uk
Phone: 08001974150

This book is a work of non-fiction. Unless otherwise noted, the author and the publisher make no explicit guarantees as to the accuracy of the information contained in this book and in some cases, names of people and places have been altered to protect their privacy. All of the stories, memories, and conversations contained in this book are based solely on the emotions, perceptions, opinions, and beliefs of the author, unless otherwise attributed to those who made written contributions to this book.

First published by AuthorHouse 2/13/2006

ISBN: 1-4259-1408-X (sc)
ISBN: 1-4259-1409-8 (dj)

Library of Congress Control Number: 2006900465

Printed in the United States of America
Bloomington, Indiana

This book is printed on acid-free paper.

DEDICATION

First and foremost, I would like thank God, who makes all things possible. I humbly dedicate this book to my role model, inspiration, best friend, and above all else my brother, Andy Cubbler. His work on Earth may very well have been completed, but his memory and legacy will live on forever in the hearts, minds, and souls of everyone who ever knew him. May this book serve as tribute to his life's work and may it serve as an inspiration to all who share in our story.

I would also like to dedicate this book to everyone who played a role in Andy's and my life. I would first like to thank our parents, Paul and Louise (Cubbler) Jones. Without their love, support, and guidance, neither Andy nor I would have grown into the men we became. You are as much a part of this book as Andy and I. It is our life story and our tribute to Andy and the life he lived. Andy and I thank you for everything that we are. To my wife, Lauren, and my two children, Rebecca and Andrew, thank you for believing in me and for loving me unconditionally. To my maternal and paternal grandparents, Alfred and Herta Linnemeier (Opa and Oma) and Roy and Mildred Cubbler (Pop-Pop and Mom-Mom), may you rest in peace knowing how much you were loved. To my step-grandparents, George and Eleanor Jones (Pop and Nan), know that you are my "blood" and I am eternally thankful for the love and support for both Andy and I.

To Darlene Atkinson (Aunt Darlene), who was not only my mom's best friend, she also was Andy's and my second parent after our dad left. I love you and may you rest in God's grace knowing that you are now free from the pain and suffering you had to endure those last few years of your life. To her daughter and her husband, Greg and Kristi Troutman, you are and will always be a part of our family. Kristi, I love you and cannot thank you enough for your constant friendship and love. Greg, you were Andy's friend at Camp Innabah and a big part of his life. I thank you for taking care of him when I could not. To Gene and Karen Troutman, thank you for loving Andy, for teaching him to be his own man, and for giving him Camp Innabah, his heaven on Earth. Gene, rest in peace knowing that your work on Earth was definitely God's work and that the fruits of your labor can be seen every single day at Camp Innabah.

To Camp Innabah and West-Mont Christian Academy, you nurtured Andy, you taught him to have confidence, and you accepted his faults and praised his accomplishments. For that, I will be eternally in your debt. May the proceeds from this book help to continue Andy's legacy of loving and caring for children through scholarships in his name at both of your fine places of love, learning, and acceptance.

To the Gilroy family (Pat, Chuck, Scott, Kelly, Chris, and Kevin), you are my other family and I thank you for treating me as one of your own. Your generosity, love, and friendship helped to ease the pain of Andy's death. You continue to be a part of my family, and for that I am thankful. To Bunk and Lynn Gladieux, I thank you for your generosity, your love, and your continued friendship. Andy would be very proud to be a part of your lives, as I certainly am. To Jane Marie (Giaquinto) Swavely, you were Andy's first and only love. Your presence in Andy's life, the impact you had, and the genuine love and friendship you showed him will forever be remembered in the hearts of our family. Andy was lucky and blessed to have had you in his life. To Russell Shaffer, who, among other things, was Mom's protector and friend, may you rest in peace and know that your life meant something to our family and that without you in our lives, we would not have been complete.

Finally, to all of Andy's friends, co-workers, teachers, and admirers, I want to personally thank you for showing me how great a person my brother truly was. My relationship with Andy, up until his death, was completely different from the individual relationships he had forged with all of you. I had no idea how amazing he was, how funny he was, or how giving he was, until I saw each and every one of you at his funeral. The love you had for Andy and the impact he had on each and every one of you was evident in your eyes, in your tears, and in your voices. You were truly one of the main inspirations for this book.

PREFACE

Life goes on—or so it is said. Why does it have to be that way? Why does a person have to "get on with their life" after they suffer a tragedy? I can't answer that question for the life of me. All I do know is that, in my case, I never actually got on with my life, at least not the life I had been leading. See, I lost my brother, Andy, in a violent car accident on July 12, 1989. From the moment I heard the news and to this day, I cannot fully comprehend why he had to die. He was special, not only to me but to everyone he ever had contact with. He was a kind, loving, forgiving, and honest person. He never was intentionally mean or hurtful; he loved all of God's creations. He went to church every Sunday, prayed every day, and lived a Christ-like life. There was no good reason to explain his sudden and violent death.

The day that he died is when my epiphany began. I cannot explain why he had to die, but I have come to realize that I do not need to know "why." It is not for me or you or anyone else to explain why God does what He does. This is what FAITH is all about. Being unable to physically see something, yet still believing that it does exist is what most religions, especially Christianity, are based on. I BELIEVE in God. I BELIEVE that He is a benevolent God. I BELIEVE that He took my brother for reasons that cannot be humanly explained or understood. I have FAITH that all things in the world happen for a reason. I also BELIEVE that God has given all of us the ability to make choices and that the results of those choices are sometimes negative.

However, for my brother, he did not make a mistake or an error in judgment. He was just in a car, driving home from work, and for some unknown reason, he became unconscious and veered into an oncoming vehicle. He did not choose this; it was chosen for him. God made the decision to bring Andy home to Him. As a result of this, I had to make a decision: be angry and hateful toward not only the world but also to God, OR accept Andy's death and have FAITH that God had other plans for Andy. I chose the latter.

My life was going forward whether or not Andy had died, but the direction my life took was significantly altered due to his death. I used Andy as an inspiration, a source of strength, and my gauge as to whether or not I am living my life as he would have lived his. I cannot be Andy, but I can use his life and his actions as a barometer to better my own life. I did not "get on with my life." I changed my course.

Chapter One

Andrew Linnemeier Cubbler was born on June 3, 1968, in suburban Philadelphia to Louise and Robert Cubbler. By all accounts, he was born "healthy" and had all his fingers and toes. But little did my mother and father know that a few years down the road, there would be many physical and emotional mountains to climb with their beautiful new son.

Andy was the first child for my mother and father. My parents met while attending Shippensburg University in Pennsylvania. My mom was sixteen years old when she started college; she skipped two grades in grade school. She majored in English and had hoped to be a teacher. She was a tall, thin, and beautiful brunette. My father was a nationally recognized wrestler in high school and he excelled at the collegiate ranks as well. He too had majored in education, with mathematics being his chosen field. He was six feet tall with red hair and a thin build. They married shortly after college and decided to start a family of their own.

My mom had a strong maternal instinct. She knew she needed to be a strong and stable mother for her son, but she also had many hopes and aspirations for him as well. Exactly one month after Andy was born, my mom came across a prayer written by General Douglas MacArthur for his own son. The prayer was so poignant for my mom that she kept it, all these years later, in a scrap book full of Andy's childhood memories. It was as if it had been written about Andy.

1

"Give me a son, O Lord, who will be strong enough to know when he is weak and brave enough to face himself when he is afraid; one who will be proud and unbending in honest defeat, and humble and gentle in victory. Build me a son whose wishes will not take the place of his deeds; a son who will know Thee—and that to know himself is the foundation stone of knowledge. Lead him, I pray, not in the path of ease and comfort, but under the stress and spur of difficulties and challenge. Here let him learn to stand up in the storm; here let him learn compassion for those who fail. Build me a son whose heart will be clear, whose goal will be high; a son who will master himself before he seeks to master other men, one who will reach into the future, yet never forget the past. And after all these things are his, add, I pray, enough of a sense of humor, so that he may always be serious but never take himself too seriously. Give him humility, so that he may always remember the simplicity of true greatness, the open mind of true wisdom, and the meekness of true strength."

The first year with Andy was typical of most newborn babies. Andy was a beautiful baby. He had blond hair, blue eyes, and a smile that could melt your heart. His actions and abilities were that of any normal baby. As far as my parents were concerned, Andy was perfect. Their dreams were simple for Andy: they hoped that he would grow up to be the type of son that they could be proud of ... a healthy, loving, and respectful young man.

Andy loved to stack blocks, sing along to *Sesame Street*, and play with his dog, a beagle named Buster Brown. Buster was Andy's first real friend. Andy loved to lie on the living room floor with Buster, who I am sure was keeping one eye open to protect the newest member of the family.

Andy had a knack for saying very difficult words for a toddler, such as "hippopotamus." The only problem was that he would never say it again. Andy, in retrospect, must have felt that he had accomplished the act of saying such a difficult word, so there was absolutely no need to keep repeating it! Andy was a very alert little boy and he always appeared to be very interested in everything that was going on around him.

My mother was a very religious woman who in turn wanted to raise her children in the church. She also had a desire to name her children after biblical characters; she especially liked the names of the twelve disciples. So when her first child was born into the world, she naturally named him Andrew, after one of the twelve disciples.

Some may wonder where Andy's middle name of Linnemeier originated. My mom was the youngest of three girls that were born to my maternal grandparents, Alfred and Herta Linnemeier. They immigrated to the United States from the town of Bremen, Germany, in 1929. My aunt Inge and aunt Ursula, my mom's sisters, were born in Germany. My mom was the only child born to my grandparents in the United States. My mom's two older sisters were fifteen and seventeen years older than she, which made for what amounted to a childhood without the benefit of siblings. Oma and Opa, the German names for grandmother and grandfather, were hard-working people. My mom was Opa's pride and joy. Opa was a very handsome and distinguished-looking man. He was six feet tall and carried a build that was the result of many years of hard, labored work. Opa was a master carpenter. He worked for many years as such and built their home from the ground up. My Opa did all the interior furniture and woodwork in solid cherry wood. Oma was your typical German "hausfrau," also known in English as a housewife. She was a little over five feet tall, but she acted as if she was much bigger. Unfortunately for her, she was diabetic and had lost her sight prior to my birth. She was a physically and mentally strong woman. She had many talents and abilities. She was not only a wonderful cook and homemaker, she could also climb up on the roof and help Opa lay beams or help to clear land for a garden.

Mom decided when Andy was born that she wanted to honor her parents and her heritage by keeping the last name in the family line. Since my Opa did not father any boys, the name would have died with him. But if you ask me, it is one hell of an inconvenience to have Linnemeier as your middle name. As if thirteen letters in your first and last names was not enough of a chore to learn, Mom had to go and throw in an extra ten letters with Linnemeier!

In April of 1971, Mom and Dad welcomed me into the fold. Andy was almost three years old when his new little brother came into the picture. Andy studied this new member of the family very closely and then decided his little brother was a great pal to take a nap with or to cuddle up with next to the dog. Almost immediately, Andy took me under his wing and protected me from harm. Up until this time, family life appeared to be going as planned for my parents: two beautiful children and a happy home.

Both my mom and dad had pursued teaching careers, but my mom stopped working to have my brother and me. From the very beginning, my mom was committed to providing Andy and me with a loving and caring life. Unfortunately for us, when Andy was almost four years old and I was one year old, my parents split up. Many years later, when Andy and I would understand, Mom explained to us why they got a divorce. She stated that my dad was a decent man but a lousy husband. She told us that she fell out of love with him. Dad, never one to show emotion, never told my mom that he loved her and never felt that marriage was something he needed to work at to make better. Mom, on the other hand, is a very outwardly emotional woman. She wears her emotions on her sleeve and is the first to tell you that she loves you. In other words, they were like oil and water—they didn't mix! Luckily for my mom, the divorce was amicable and my dad did not contest any portion of the divorce proceedings.

However, my dad moving out of the house left my mom home alone with two young children. My father leaving was probably not in my mom's plan when she decided to get pregnant and put her career on hold. However, my mom was a fighter and a survivor, and she knew that she had to fight to make our lives as good as possible.

Mom began to work multiple jobs to keep food on the table and a roof over our head. The first job I remember my mom having was as a cocktail waitress at the local Holiday Inn. She would always take me out to lunch (pea soup) at the restaurant before she began her 8 p.m. to 2 a.m. shift at the bar. Knowing my mom as well as I do today, a cocktail waitress is the last job I would have imagined her having! My mom is a natural klutz! She often trips and falls down for no reason and I still can't imagine why she excelled at this profession. But she was very good at serving drinks and she always used to tell me that she could remember every regular customer's "usual" drink. While our neighbor girl baby-sat, my mom worked nights to be able to be home with us during the days. Plus, her good tips helped to keep Andy and I fed and warm.

Our neighbor Darlene was another single mom and she helped Mom get that Holiday Inn job. Mom, trusting only her instincts for "good character," allowed herself to become close friends with "Aunt Darlene." Aunt Darlene was a beautiful, slender blonde who, according to my mom, had no troubles being noticed by all the guys. Their friendship grew at a rather quick pace, mostly because they shared so many of the same qualities. They were both single mom's, with two kids, and they were strong-willed and loving people. During the summer when I was two years old, Mom asked Aunt Darlene to share expenses for a week at Rehoboth Beach, Delaware, a beach community. Darlene accepted. She and her two children, Billy and Kristi, had never even seen the ocean. It was a trip that would begin the saga of the "Mighty Moms." This was the beginning of a lifelong friendship and a surrogate family for both of our families.

In 1972 and 1973, Andy began to go to preschool and I was in day care while Mom worked her two jobs. Andy was still progressing well for his age and all seemed to be going as expected during this time in his life. I can remember spending time out in the yard, playing with Andy and wondering when would I grow up and be just like him. I looked up to him. Even though I was only two years old, I knew he was my older

5

brother. He always was there to keep an eye on me. He always held my hand when we crossed the street and always pointed out to me all the hazards in the yard and what to touch and what not to touch inside the house. He was my boss and I listened like a good little employee!

The worst nightmare for a parent nearly happened when I was three years old and Andy was five years old. Andy almost died as a result of an allergic reaction to a bee sting. We were out in the front yard playing army. We used sticks to serve as our swords and guns, and we made believe that we were U.S. soldiers fighting a war against an invisible enemy.

While playing, we found a mud nest in the ground where a large tree had once lived. Being young and adventurous, we decided to do what normal boys do ... we poked it with our "swords"! We had no idea what was living inside this mud nest, but we soon found out. As we continued to explore this new "enemy fortress," Andy decided that the hose would be a great weapon to use to oust the enemy. We began to spray the nest and this definitely angered the creatures that lived within the fortresses walls. Bees! Not just a few bees, but a whole freaking army of them! They swarmed and swarmed and we continued to try to fight them off with the hose.

Unfortunately for Andy and me, we had no idea how much this was actually pissing off the bees. Andy and I both got stung multiple times. We ran into the house screaming for help from Mom. When we got inside and away from the bees, Mom noticed Andy's eye was red and beginning to swell. He had been stung multiple times in the eye by the swarming bees.

At this point in Andy's life, a bee had never stung him. Mom soon noticed that Andy's whole face had begun to swell and he was having difficulty breathing. Mom recognized that this was indeed NOT a normal reaction and took him to the nearby hospital. Once in the emergency room, Andy's situation began to worsen. The doctors gave Andy medication to reverse the obvious allergic reaction to the bee stings. However, Andy stopped breathing. The doctors worked feverishly to resuscitate him and after several minutes without taking a single breath, Andy finally began breathing again. Needless to say, Mom was very scared and terrified that her firstborn son, at the age of five years old, might die. Once Andy's breathing became regular and the anti-bee sting medication took hold, he started to stabilize. Thank the Lord!

During the early years, we had a lot of friendly people around to help us out. However, this was an extremely difficult time in my family's life. Bills got to be too much for my mom to handle, so we had to sell the house and move into an apartment complex about a mile away. Aunt Darlene and her two kids, Kristi and Billy, still lived across the street from our old house, but we still stayed in daily contact. Having Aunt Darlene as a friend made life a little easier for my mom, since she had someone nearby to talk to and we often shared meals together as well. After a while, it was as if we were one big happy family. The six of us were inseparable. We slept over at each others' houses and that first vacation together to Rehoboth became a ritual. We had two "Mighty Moms" and life began to feel normal for us.

On one of our visits to Aunt Darlene's house after we had moved, Andy, Billy, Kristi, and I were playing outside in the yard. Mom and Aunt Darlene had just bought us all new pairs of "Bo-Bo" sneakers. "Bo-Bo" sneakers were what we called cheap sneakers that you buy from the bin at the supermarket. They were brightly colored, canvas sneakers with the large rubber toes on the outside. At the time, this was all they could afford to buy us. It had rained the day before and the property next door to their house was nothing but mud. At this time in our lives, Billy was the ringleader. He thought it would be a good idea to play in the mud while wearing our new sneakers. We had a blast, but when we returned to the house with our completely muddy shoes, my mom flipped!

Back in those days, corporal punishment was an acceptable form of discipline. My mom's method of choice was the now-infamous wooden spoon. After attending church one Sunday morning and hearing the pastor give a sermon about "hands should never be used for hitting," she made the decision to use the wooden spoon as her method of delivery, rather than the hand. She never hit us hard with it, but the fear of getting a hard whack to the rear end was devastating to Andy and me. After seeing our muddy sneakers, Mom retrieved some of Aunt Darlene's wooden spoons from the kitchen. Being the only girl, Kristi always got a lighter version of the punishment. Mom usually chose the first recipient by their age, youngest to oldest. Mom told us all to drop our pants to our knees and bend over. I was first to receive my spanking. Having been a recipient of the dreaded wooden spoon before, I knew that crying after the first whack was the best way to get out of multiple whacks. So, after my first whack, out came the tears! Worked every time! Kristi was next. She had been crying ever since my mom told us she was getting the wooden spoons! One light whack to the butt was all she would receive. Andy was third in line. He never really cried a whole lot. Mom whacked him on the butt and he stood there stoically. Mom, knowing how he reacted to such things, did not take this as an act of defiance and let him go with the one whack to the butt.

Billy, on the other hand, was older and already had an attitude problem. Mom let him have his first whack and he didn't flinch. Mom gave him two more and he responded with, "That didn't even hurt!" That was the wrong thing to say to my mom. My mom might have been a God-fearing, Christian woman, but she was not one to be shown up, especially not by one of us kids! She hit him again, but this time a little harder, and the handle of the spoon broke. Billy, not known for being the most astute boy, still would not let out a tear or a whimper. Mom, not to be defeated, retrieved a second spoon. She broke this one as well. I don't remember how long this battle of wills went on, but legend has it that Billy's rear end withstood multiple whacks from five different wooden spoons! Needless to say, Aunt Darlene needed to buy more of those after this particular day!

To Mom and Aunt Darlene, we were a family now. This included all the good and sometimes the hard times that go along with being a family. Disciplining the kids was part of their responsibility as parents. However, as far as we were concerned, we could have done without that part of the whole family equation!

The only thing in Andy's and my life that did not feel normal was our relationship with our dad. After my dad left, he and my mom set up a visitation schedule and he began to pay child support. Dad would come on Saturdays to pick us up and take us to our grandmother's house, where he was living. Mom-Mom was the greatest grandmother a kid could ever wish for. My grandfather, Pop-Pop died when I was nine months old. I never really got a chance to get to know him, but Mom-Mom made sure Andy and I knew all the stories and all the memories she had of him and how he felt when we were born. We always referred to Pop-Pop as "Pop-Pop in heaven" whenever we spoke about him.

Mom-Mom was a fantastic woman. In her younger days, she looked like a movie star. She had auburn hair, perfect skin, and a smile that made men fall at her feet. She was still a beautiful woman when I was a kid; however, she now had gray hair and not-so-perfect skin! Mom-Mom was a true kid at heart. She used to love to play with us and she made Andy and me feel very special even though our dad made no attempt to make us feel that way. She made up cool games and told so many stories that I am sure were more fantasy than they were reality. Andy and I always felt that although we loved to be with Mom-Mom, this was supposed to be our time with Dad.

Unfortunately, on most occasions, he would just sleep in his room all day long. On the rare occasion that he actually was awake and did something with us, he usually cut it short and took us home early. Looking back on it now, I think he was out late the night before our visits, revisiting his youth, so to speak. My dad was not a bad guy and he never hit us or yelled at us. He just seemed indifferent to Andy and me. Nothing we did would make him show any type of emotion. This feeling of wanting to be noticed and loved would haunt Andy and me for many years to come.

CHAPTER TWO

When Andy turned six years old something changed inside him. Andy began to stutter. During the early 1970s, the cause for why people stutter was as unclear as the agreed-upon treatment. Andy's stutter was a speech impediment that was different from the usual ones that some children experience, such as having a lisp or having trouble correctly pronouncing one's R's. Andy did not have one specific sound that he could not say and there was no predictable pattern. With certain people and in certain situations Andy did not stutter too much, but the problem did not go away, and a difficult year in kindergarten made matters worse.

Andy was a happy child who often hummed while he worked, and he saw the world in Technicolor and so colored accordingly—much to his teacher's dismay. My mom got so worried that she took Andy to a counselor to see if the divorce had somehow caused Andy to stutter. The counselor met with my mom, dad, and Andy. The counselor recommended that Andy begin "play therapy" to work out what he couldn't explain in words. The school district, on the other hand, placed him in a pre-first-grade class for students that were not emotionally ready for first grade. My mom, wanting to do what was best for Andy, agreed to send him there.

After a short while at the school, my mom had her first parent-teacher conference with his teacher. The teacher wanted to know the reasons why Andy was placed in her class. She stated that Andy was functioning well and she could not find any reason for him to be in her class. Andy was transferred out of that class and into a classroom for those without special needs. This was short lived, but it was a big relief for my mom.

Over the next couple of years, Andy and I grew ever closer as brothers and playmates. On the school front, life seemed to progress rather well. He was learning at the rate of other normal children, but he still was struggling with his stutter. Not a day went by in which he did not have to deal with a situation that caused his stuttering to get in the way of interacting well with others.

In fourth grade it appeared that things were finally starting to go Andy's way for once. He was rather tall for his age and pencil thin. He was definitely feeling better about himself, but one thing neither of us felt good about was our horrible haircuts! My mom took a liking to cutting our hair at home, since money was tight. Unfortunately for Andy and me, the scissors and the dreaded thinning shears my mom had were from a generation long ago and probably had never been sharpened since the day they were made. Mom also preferred her two sons to wear the "Dutch Boy"-style haircut. We liked to refer to it as the "bowl" cut! For most of our early childhood, we wore this style of haircut. I think Mom chose this style because it was the easiest to cut, and no matter how crooked our bangs might have been it didn't really matter too much. The uneven bangs lent themselves to the "bowl" haircut perfectly.

Not all of my memories about our childhood involved my brother. I do remember one memory that was more of a solo act rather than one in tandem. In 1977, around Halloween time, I had my first of many life-threatening incidents. We were living in the apartment complex we moved to after Mom had to sell the house. Up the street from our apartment was an entranceway to another complex. Having recently seen the first *Superman* movie, starring Christopher Reeve, I actually believed that I too had super powers. I decided to climb the tree that was right next to the street and the entranceway to the other apartment complex. I climbed to the top of the tree, thinking that I too could fly just like Superman. So, naturally, I jumped!

I actually had every intention of flying through the air, swooping down on my mortal enemies, and saving the day for all mankind. But instead, I landed on the macadam parking lot and cracked my skull. I remember running home crying; unbeknownst to my mom, I had suffered a severe head injury. She asked me what I had done wrong. (I was a six-year-old boy and was known to cause some trouble!) I told her I couldn't remember and she sent me to my room. It wasn't until a neighborhood kid came by to ask if I was okay that she realized something was truly wrong. She rushed me to the hospital and I remained there for a few days, recovering from my bout of stupidity. My mom stayed up all night with me every night. She cross-stitched a blanket for me while she watched over me in the hospital. To this day, it is a reminder of the commitment and love she had for Andy and me. In retrospect, I wonder if it was me who actually had a learning disability and not Andy!

We lived in that apartment for a couple of years. When I was about to enter the third grade, my mom started working in real estate. Part of her salary was a "free" townhouse in a new school district. My mom took Andy to his new elementary school to find out how they were going to assist her with Andy's growth in school. Having read Andy's school reports from his other school, they decided to give Andy a standard IQ test so they could better understand where he was intellectually. Andy tested terribly. He scored so low that he was deemed extremely learning disabled/borderline mentally retarded. My mom was told that he would never be able to function in the world alone—never get a job, drive a car, or do anything that those with normal intelligence could do without effort.

These "professionals" thought it best to put him in a class for the learning disabled. The class was a rough group of kids who threw desks and threatened and taunted Andy.

Unlike those kids, Andy did not have a mean bone in his body. He would come home so frustrated from being picked on by kids who equated stuttering with mental retardation ... and the name-calling began. He would punch the wall or the bed, screaming, "I am not retarded!" These "professionals" could not see that Andy was not mentally retarded; he was just a frightened little boy who could not find a way to communicate his feelings with others for fear of being ridiculed. He was so afraid to fail that he subconsciously caused himself to do just that.

Every day that Andy spent in that class was another day of torture for him. This was the first time in Andy's life that he saw the evil in people. He was called a "retard" and a "moron," and they relentlessly mimicked his stuttering, to the point where Andy just stopped talking at school. This didn't help him at all, but his defense mechanism to combat his aggressors was to just shut down completely. This repetitive trauma continued throughout the year. Unfortunately for Mom, she felt helpless. She could not seem to find a school for Andy that would actually take an active role in his learning development. He needed extra attention from teachers, and up until this time he was getting none.

Living in our new "free" townhouse was initially very exciting. This place was a little bigger and it had a basement, which Andy and I thought was cool! Shortly after moving there, Darlene and her kids moved in across the street. During the couple of years that we resided there, my relationship with Andy began to blossom into what it would become later on in our lives.

The kids that lived in the development were not very friendly. This is the time in Andy's life when he began to experience the meanness in people outside of the classroom and the onslaught of name-calling that he had to endure. This is also when our relationship began to change. Up until this time, I was Andy's little brother. However, once we started to play with these neighborhood kids, I think we switched roles. I had a hard time dealing with these kids picking on my brother. They would call him a "retard" and would mimic him when he stuttered. It got to the point that I had to step in and stop them.

I got into a lot of fights during the two years that we lived there. Andy would never fight. He would take all their words and actions and shrug them off. I would always ask him why he didn't get mad and punch them in the face and he would say, "Those kids are the ones who are stupid." Once again, Andy took the high road instead letting them see how much their words actually hurt him.

I was now acting out the role of the stereotypical "older brother." Since Andy refused to stand up to the bullies in the neighborhood, I decided that I was not going to allow them to get away with saying such horrible things about MY brother! I fought and I fought, hoping that they would leave him alone. Every day after school, I had to fight. At the time, with the little life experience I had, I thought that if I stood up to them by fighting them that they would leave Andy alone. All I accomplished was a lot of bloody noses and bloody lips. I guess Andy's choice to ignore them was just as effective as my path of fighting. Unfortunately, I only recently figured this out, so I continued to fight for Andy's right to a normal life, free from name-calling and the mimicking of his stutter.

By the time Andy was in fifth grade, my mom had returned to teaching. The educator in her knew that no child should go through this much agony in school. She was a good friend with the guidance counselor at her school. He told my mom that he had an older brother who had struggled in school as well. That brother would eventually grow up to become a maintenance man, marry and have kids, and live a very happy life. The counselor told her some advice that would equip my mom to "fight for Andy" all her life. He told her, "No one knows your son better than you. Don't let any school put a label on him that you know is not the truth. Fight for him! You are your son's best advocate."

Mom took this advice and once again sought outside professional help at a mental health clinic. The psychologist there tested Andy and met with him for a few months. This psychologist seemed to take an actual interest in Andy and he was driven to find out what was going on in his mind. He was the first "professional" to actually try to figure Andy out. All the prior "professionals" either lacked the knowledge needed to diagnose Andy's condition or were just collecting our money and going through the motions with Andy. This psychologist had a completely different diagnosis than the one prior to him. His conclusion was that ANDY HAD NORMAL OR ABOVE-AVERAGE INTELLIGENCE BUT HE WAS LIKE A PITCHER OF WATER WITH A LID ON IT AND HE REALLY COULD NOT SEE HOW TO GET THAT LID OFF. It would prove to be a diagnosis that was all too true. Andy, who so wanted to achieve excellence, would struggle to learn, fall into a pattern of lying about low grades, pay the emotional price when report cards or teacher phone calls came, and always would feel like he wasn't "good enough." Little did Andy know at the time that he would someday prove all his critics wrong.

During these early years is when I first remember Mom's mentally retard friend, Russell. She had worked with him at the Holiday Inn and he quickly took a liking to Mom. He was in his early fifties when they met and had recently been sent out into the world when the group home he was living in had closed. He liked my mom mostly because she did not treat him as if he were mentally retarded. Growing up, I can remember my many phone conversations with Russell … about ten per day! He used to call all the time. I think he would forget that he called earlier in the day. I remember this gentle, gravel-voiced man calling and asking for "Maweez," as he called my mom. For some reason "Louise" was a name he could not pronounce. If you ask me, it reminded me of "Weezie" from the TV Sitcom *The Jeffersons*, so I kinda liked it!

On the occasions that Mom was too tired to talk to him or had told him everything she needed to the other nine times he had called, we'd have to cover for her. We used to make up excuses for why she couldn't talk to him. The most frequently used excuse was the one where we told him that she had gone to the store to buy ice cream. This ended up being a running joke between Russell and my family. This would make Russell laugh aloud when we told him that she had gone to the store to buy MORE ice cream! He'd typically respond with the familiar line, "She'd better watch out or she'll turn into a heavyweight!" Anyways, from that point on, he'd ask for my mom when he called and refer to her as "the heavyweight."

As you can probably imagine, when Andy would answer the phone the conversation with Russell was almost comical. Andy would answer the phone with a clear, "Hello," but everything that followed was one long stuttering session. Couple Andy's stuttering with Russell's inability to understand a whole lot and you have a phone conversation for the record books! Andy would make an attempt to talk slowly and he would try with all his might to speak without stuttering, but it rarely happened. Russell was a patient man and I don't really think that Andy's stuttering bothered him one bit. After a while, I'd take the phone from Andy for the simple reason that if I had let it go on much longer, no one else would ever get through to our house! As far as my mom being a "heavyweight," she was very thin for most of my childhood! Russell liked to kid her that she would get too fat eating all that ice cream, so the name sort of stuck. Up until the day I moved out of the house, Russell called every day and still called her the "heavyweight"!

CHAPTER THREE

As I tried to collect all the memories I had of my brother, I found it easy to remember them but difficult to narrow down the choices to a select few that would end up in the book. Instead of choosing myself which memories to use, I asked for Andy's divine help and I let my mind wander through the vast collection of memories I had locked away for so many years.

Early on in our relationship, I looked to Andy for guidance and I looked up to him as my older brother. I used to follow him around the house, mimicking his actions and hoping he'd notice me. I was your typical little brother. I seemed to get myself into trouble frequently. Andy always warned me to stop what I was doing, but of course, I'd never listen! After getting yelled at by Mom, Andy would come over to me and say, "Matt, I told you not to do that!" Now, mind you, there were many stuttered words in that one sentence, but the meaning was crystal clear.

Once Andy's stutter became more frequent, I developed an ability to "decode" his stutter. I was actually able to finish his sentences for him when he was having a really hard time talking. It probably was not helping him overcome his stutter, but I wanted to ease his agony. When Andy was stuttering really badly, his face would become contorted and his eyes would roll back into his head. He knew what he looked like when this happened and he would be so embarrassed when it did. I hated to see him struggle with simple phrases. He hated being a stutterer, and I hated seeing him in so much pain, so I decided that if I could decipher what he wanted to say, I'd say it for him. Usually I was right on target with my translations, and when I got it right, Andy would always say, "Thanks, bro!"

Another thing that Andy and I shared from the time we were very little until we were both in our late teens was the "good-night ritual." Every night when we went to bed, Andy would yell from his room, "See you in the morning, Matt!" I, of course, replied in kind. Then Andy would follow that up with, "I love you, bro!"

Needless to say, I'd reply with, "I love you too, Andy!" To this day, I miss that little ritual.

Our vacations to Rehoboth Beach were looked forward to every year. We loved to go away with Aunt Darlene, Kristi, and Billy.

One summer in particular produced one of those memorable trips in the car on the way to the beach. Just about every parent has had one of those family vacations where he or she drives to their destination, and during that trip in the family car, the kids inevitably argue and fight and continually ask, "Are we there yet?" This particular trip in the family car to Rehoboth Beach was one of those dreadful occasions. At the time, my mom owned what we affectionately called "The Blue Bomber." This was a monstrosity of a vehicle! It was a four-door car large enough to fit all four kids, Mom, Aunt Darlene, and all our luggage with room to spare! The trip to Rehoboth took a little over four hours by car. We were sitting in the back seat and acting like kids—pulling hair, yelling, whining, and bickering with each other! This seemed to really annoy Aunt Darlene after a while. She warned us several times to stop fighting … OR ELSE!

Well, "or else" happened on the side of the highway! She told Mom to pull over and she proceeded to pull all four of us out of the car. One by one, she worked her way down the line, giving each of us a swift smack on the rear end! She didn't care who saw her, she did it right out in the open for all the passing cars to see. She was so fed up with our antics that she had to take care of business right then and there! She then ordered us back into the car and we drove the rest of the way in silence! Good thing for us kids that Aunt Darlene and Mom had very short memories; they soon forgot all about the incident.

When we were still young, Andy and I would spend hours playing wiffle ball on the beach. We were always on the same team and the two of us together were a formidable foe! Andy was the speed and I was the skill. It worked out so well that we started to get picked by the older kids to be on their teams!

Those early trips to the shore were some of the greatest times ever. The four of us would hang out at the beach or in the old boarding house we rented and play card games and watch TV. At night, we would go to "Funland" on the boardwalk and play video games, ride amusement rides, and eat tons of cotton candy. Andy loved to play Pac-Man. He was very good at it and used to challenge me to see who was the best. I rarely got the best of him; for a "learning disabled" kid, he has very "able" at this task! God, I wish I could go back in time and be that little kid again with Andy, Kristi, and Billy. Those days are sorely missed!

When we were young, while Mom was working so much to support us, Andy and I spent most evenings with a baby-sitter. The one who watched us the most was Margie. Knowing about life as I do today, she would be classified as a hippie lesbian who had a knack for playing folk music on the guitar. Every night was a mini-Woodstock when she would watch us! When she baby-sat us, she would bring her guitar and teach us songs. We learned how to play "Leaving on a Jet Plane." She tried to teach us other songs, but for some reason, Andy always wanted to play that particular song. However, after a while, we grew tired of the "peace and love fest" and began wanting to see Mom.

My mom would usually be home from work at midnight. Andy and I would insist on waiting up for her or we slept on the couch so we could say good night. My mom worked so hard as a waitress and at the mini-mart that her legs would ache from being on her feet for so long. On many occasions, Mom would lie down on the couch and Andy and I would both sit on her legs. For whatever reason, this seemed to make her legs feel better. I must admit, though, that our intentions were a little skewed. Mom would always give us a candy bar for sitting on her legs!

Throughout our childhood, Andy and I spent most of our time together. Andy was about ten years old and I was seven or eight years old when we were old enough to play team sports. Team athletics came naturally to me. Andy, on the other hand, was not a real extrovert and the concept of "team sports" was never his forte! Andy had one thing I did not: he could run like the wind and could do so for what seemed to be forever. I, on the other hand, was skilled at hitting and fielding a baseball but ran like I had a safe on my back!

Andy and I played soccer when we were younger. Neither Andy nor I really got into it too much. Andy never really got the concept of what direction to kick the ball and I never got the concept of playing a sport that required you to run for miles. Not to mention that when it was all said and done, the score was a 0-0 tie!

Baseball was the next sport we both decided to play. I finally found a sport that required me to run only ninety feet, and I really enjoyed hitting and fielding the ball. Andy probably would have excelled in baseball too, had he played it long enough to do so. The last game of Andy's baseball career was one of the first games he played in. Andy was playing the outfield and a ball got hit in the air toward him. Instead of catching the ball with his glove, he took a direct hit to that area just south of the belly button! Andy calmly walked off the field before the inning was over. He walked over to my mom and, in one of the rare times in his life when he spoke a clear and understandable phrase, said, "I quit!" That was the end of that sport for him!

In 1980, we moved into a split-level home. We lived on the top floor and a guy named "J. J." lived beneath us. This was the first house we had ever lived in that had a driveway. "J. J." was a single guy who drove a Pontiac Trans Am. He was your typical "gigolo" kind of guy: the butterfly-collared shirt open to the middle of his chest, gold necklaces, and of course, that Trans Am. Andy and I got a kick out him and we used to watch out our bedroom window as a different young lady was brought into his place every weekend! He never really liked us, mostly because we kept hitting his car with tennis balls, basketballs, and on one occasion, a baseball. Kids will be kids, though.

During the transition from the townhouse to the new house, my mom and Aunt Darlene would go back to the townhouse to remove more items to bring to the new house. About a week after we moved into the new house, my mom had decided to go back and clean the townhouse. She wanted it to look nice for the new people who would be renting it after us. Mom headed over to clean, and when she got there she tried to unlock to door to go inside. However, the inside chain lock was on and she could not get in. This had my mom baffled for a few minutes. My mom is a very smart woman. However, the simple things can kind of seem like molecular physics! She stood there for a while, wondering how she could have placed the chain lock on the door when she was last at the house. It never occurred to her that someone might actually be inside the house. Luckily, as divine intervention would have it, Aunt Darlene showed up out of the blue. She thought Mom might be there and thought she might need a helping hand. Mom explained the chain-lock situation and Aunt Darlene knew immediately what was going on … a burglar!

Aunt Darlene had amazing instincts and was street savvy. She took control of the situation, with Mom looking on in disbelief. She ran to the back of the house to the sliding glass door. She checked to see if it was unlocked and it was.

She carefully slid the door open and made an announcement to whoever was inside the house. She yelled inside, "This is the police, we have the place surrounded!" Mom went to the neighbor's house and called the police. They arrived on the scene just as the eighteen-year-old emerged from the basement. According to the police, he had been kicked out of his house and had seen us moving out earlier in the week. He figured that it would be a safe place to hang out until he figured out what he was going to do next. In today's day and age, what Aunt Darlene did that day could have turned out badly. However, I had to hand it to her: she had a ton of guts!

That same year we also got our first basketball net for us to practice on. Andy would go out first thing in the morning and start shooting hoops. I would go out there with him, but I was still kind of short and stocky and that net seemed very high at the time. Andy seemed to pick up the art of the jump shot quite easily. We'd play games of "H.O.R.S.E." to kill time. For those of you who never played "H.O.R.S.E.," it is a game in which you create your own shot and the other player has to mimic it correctly. The player who does not make the correct shot gets a letter. The first player to get all five letters that spell "H.O.R.S.E." is the loser. Needless to say, Andy would step back for a long jump shot and make almost all of them. I, on the other hand, could only do a lay-up and so wound up losing every game until I was about sixteen years old!

Every Sunday was reserved for church. I don't think we missed a Sunday sermon until I was old enough to get a job! One of the great things about going to church when we were little was coming home to watch professional wrestling on TV! Mom was not a fan of this fine show of athletics at its best. She basically banned us from watching it. But Andy was pretty slick about watching it without Mom knowing. When Mom was in the kitchen making lunch, we would turn on the TV and have the volume down so low that you could only hear it if you were up close to the TV. I served as the lookout to make sure Mom did not come into the living room and catch us! Andy would sit about two inches from the TV so he could hear the announcer talk about the match. He loved to watch Hulk Hogan, Andre "the Giant," Jimmy "Superfly" Snuka, and all the other greats from the past. Ah, those were the days!

Andy and I were also avid football fans—we bled Philadelphia Eagles green! Another one of our favorite indoor games that we played was called "Over the Top." This game simulated a goal-line stand in a football game, where the running back would jump over the defensive linemen into the end zone. We would alternate turns on offense and defense. The goal of the game was to run down the hallway and into our bedroom. The one on defense would stand in a "three-point stance" in front of the bed, and when the offensive player came into the bedroom, he would jump over the other player. The defensive player would then flip the runner over him and onto the bed. For the most part, landing on the bed was accomplished; however, there were times when the offensive player would get launched a little too far and into the wall. Ouch!

Looking back on my childhood with my brother, I really can't believe we did not get seriously hurt. We had wild imaginations and those imaginations sometimes got the best of us. One thing that was never in question was that we had a blast coming up with some of those games!

Mom with Andy when he was about one year old.

Andy with his German stuffed bear in front of the house
when he was eighteen months old.

Andy keeping watch over his new little brother, me.

"Best Friends." Andy age five and me age two.

"Mighty Moms" and the kids in 1975. *Clockwise from the top:*
Aunt Darlene, Mom, Andy, me, Kristi, and Billy.

All the kids on one of our annual trips to Rehoboth Beach,
Delaware. *Left to right:* Billy, Andy, Kristi, and me.

Andy receives a new stuffed bear named "Uno,"
Christmas 1974.

Andy's third-grade school picture.

CHAPTER FOUR

The year we moved into our new house, my dad remarried. Through the eyes of a ten-year-old boy, his new wife, Janet, seemed intolerant and harsh. That is not to say that this was her true personality; it was just the way it appeared through my own eyes at that time. She never took the time to get to know Andy or me. She was much younger than my dad was and she did not seem to want Andy or me around. She would say very hurtful and mean things to Andy and me. She would say things such as she was glad we were not her kids and that since she was now married to Dad, we would have to deal with her.

She also appeared to be very jealous of the fact that my mom and dad had children and she did not have any of her own. It also seemed to me that she was also in total control of my dad's life. If she did not want us around on a weekend we were scheduled to be with our dad, he would call and cancel our visit.

I can remember one occasion when she came right out and said that she hated us. I was about twelve years old and she had just smacked me across the face for doing something "wrong." I was in the other room crying and my dad came in and asked what had happened. I told him that Janet had smacked me across the face and he went into the kitchen to ask her why she did it. I could hear them talking and she told my dad that she hated us and wished we would never come back.

As per the usual, my dad did not defend us in any way, shape, or form. He just tried to console Janet and he totally forgot that I was in the other room crying, hoping that he would come in and comfort me! This was par for the course when it came to my father. One big letdown!

Around this same time, my mom began dating a fellow by the name of Paul Jones. On the night that they met, my mom and a friend went out for a "girls' night" at the Holiday Inn where Mom used to wait tables. Andy and I stayed at home with a sitter. Mom really needed the night out. The band that was playing at the lounge was called Emerald City. They were your typical late-'70s-early-'80s rock-and-roll band; they played some of the great hits by the Doobie Brothers and Earth, Wind, and Fire. Paul was the drummer in the band. My mom and her friend had a good view of the band and were enjoying themselves immensely. However, Mom always worried about Andy and me when she was not home. She made frequent calls home just to make sure everything was okay.

During one of the band's "sets," my mom saw Paul do this thing with his drumsticks … she called it a "twirl." He then pointed the drumsticks at my mom; I assume it was a cool drummer thing to do at that time! After the band finished their set, Paul came up to my mom and asked her out. My mom told him something to the effect of, "I am a single mother of two boys and I do not have the time or the energy to date at this time!" I don't think my mom was very persuasive, since Paul came to the house the next night to take her to a George Benson concert!

Mom dated occasionally throughout the years after she and Dad divorced. Mom, Andy, and I were a close family. Mom had a rule about the men she dated: she would not date anyone that Andy and I did not approve of or like. I can remember the routine as if it was yesterday. My mom brought a date into the house, usually on the second or third date, to meet Andy and me. We'd talk for a while, feeling one another out. This would last about fifteen to twenty minutes, and then Mom would come into the room and tell us it was time for them to leave for their date. When she returned home from her date, she would say, "Well? What do you guys think of him?" Andy and I would tell her one of two things: either we liked him or he was a "schmuck"! That was our word for a guy we didn't like. Trust me, there were plenty of "schmucks," but there were a few we liked and she'd date them. Most of the time, being a mother of two boys was not the right ingredient for a long-term relationship, so all of the prior men in Mom's life usually left before things got too serious.

But not Paul Jones; he stayed. We gave Mom the green light to continue dating him and surprisingly he continued coming back. Looking back on it now, I am pretty sure Andy and I were to blame for my mom's failed relationships, but she would never, ever admit to that in a million years. Always protecting her boys—that was what she lived for! Paul was the first one to jump into our life with both feet, regardless of what Andy or I did to make it a less-than-attractive situation.

This, as it turned out, was the beginning of our new life as a "real family." About two months into their courtship, my mom almost died from an asthma attack. We were sitting in the house and she was having difficulty breathing. She had suffered from asthma for a long time and we were used to Mom and her asthma attacks. But this one was different. She was really struggling. I called an ambulance and they took us all to the emergency room. Mom was so bad that they had to admit her into the hospital. This situation created another situation for Andy and me. We needed someone to watch over us while she was in the hospital.

Mom decided that her only hope was for Paul to stay at the house to make sure we were fed, bathed, and in school. This was a giant leap of faith for her. She had only known him for a couple of months, but she was a good judge of character. She trusted him and in turn so did Andy and I. Those two weeks were different from any other two weeks in our lives. Besides worrying about Mom, we had this strange dude taking care of us. He tried to keep things as normal as possible for us. He cooked (not his strong suit) and cleaned. He made sure we did our homework and he played catch in the yard with us. He was actually pretty cool.

By the time the two weeks were over, Mom was feeling better and was allowed to come home from the hospital. Paul had the house perfectly maintained and he even cleaned out the lint filter in the dryer. According to Paul, there was enough lint in the filter to catch the house on fire and make a nice afghan for us to snuggle up with on cold nights! Mom, not known for her mechanical prowess, had no clue that there was a filter on the dryer. It seemed like Paul might actually come in handy.

Mom and Paul dated for about a year before they got engaged and then married. Paul left his life as a "rock star" and turned in his "butterfly-collar" shirt for one worn by preachers. Yes, it is true ... rock star to preacher; I was a little skeptical myself! For the next few years, Paul worked full-time during the day and went to seminary school at nights.

Things were not always rosy in our new family. It had always been Mom, Andy, and me and we had our own ways of dealing with things. Paul, who was only twenty-six when they began dating and eleven years younger than my mom, was not accustomed to having two pre-teen boys in his life. Paul was a disciplinarian. Not to say that Mom wasn't, but their styles differed completely. Before Paul came into the picture, the rule of the house was that if you had to get something off your chest, you did so without repercussions. Basically, Andy and I could say whatever we had to and Mom would listen and we would not get mad or hold grudges. I, more so than Andy, took advantage of this rule. I was what most adults would call a "smart ass"!

Paul's approach was more of the dictatorship style ... MY WAY OR THE HIGHWAY. As you could probably imagine, being a ten-year-old boy, this was not an easy transition for me. This is not to say that we were not happy; we just had to adjust. Andy adjusted quite easily, since he was not one to cause confrontation. I, on the other hand, took a little while longer to get with the program. From a very early age, I think

I had this desire to be in control of my life. With the three of us, I had a lot of freedom to make decisions. Mom trusted our instincts and her method of parenting was working well. With Paul now in the fold, he defrocked me of my ability to exercise that freedom. There were new rules and regulations to obey and I fought them tooth and nail! But, looking back on it as an adult, our life was better with Paul in our lives. We had two incomes, a two-parent household, and a lot of love. But Andy still had to deal with his struggle with stuttering and all the baggage that went with it.

My mom remarrying was a blessing, but it also caused a lot of stress for Andy and me. Up until this time in our lives, we only had a part-time relationship with our father. Our relationship was predicated solely on my dad's desire to see us. We would usually call him on Friday to see what time he was coming to pick us up on Saturday. You would think that if you were a father separated from your two sons, it would be you who would call to find this information out, but that wasn't my dad. On many occasions, we would call and he would come up with some excuse as to why he could not come to get us that particular weekend. More often than not, we'd go several weeks without seeing him or hearing from him.

I remember Andy and me crying on the phone with our dad, pleading for him to come and see us. My dad appeared as unemotional as any person could be. He seemed to never show any kind of emotion. Andy and I tried so hard to get him to say something, positive or negative. As I said before, at least from our perspective, he was indifferent to us.

We used to get into trouble on purpose just to get him to notice us. Even then, he would talk to us as if we were one of his students in school. His tone was very cold and unfeeling. We were waiting for him to send to the principal's office or give us a detention slip. Nothing ever seemed to faze him. My mom would say that this was just his personality.

My mom told me a story once that summed up my dad in a nutshell: When they were dating in college, he had a car that was basically a piece of junk. She recalled on one occasion, the car was burning oil and a large cloud of smoke was spewing out of the tail pipe. Rather than pull over to find the cause of the problem or take it to a mechanic, my dad decided to remove the rearview mirror so he did not have to look at the smoke pouring out of the exhaust! That was Dad: ignore and look the other way, hoping that either it would go away or he'd forget about the problem! That is the way he treated Andy, and to a lesser degree, me as well. True to form, Mom would still defend him in front of us. She tried to tell us that he did in fact love us, deep down in his soul, but to a kid that meant absolutely nothing.

Now that Paul was going to be our stepfather, we were very confused as to what to call him. Luckily for us, he said that "Paul" would be just fine. He did not try to take the place of our nonexistent father. He was very good about not getting too involved where the issue of our dad was concerned. This, however, I think caused Andy and me to crave attention from our father even more. I guess we both hoped that he might feel threatened by Paul's presence in our lives. We hoped he would start to come and see us more often and take a more active role in our lives. Needless to say, he didn't. If anything, he might have been relieved. I remember him saying that Paul was a nice guy and that we should treat him like a dad. He really seemed intent on that feeling. Looking back on it now, I can see how the frequency and length of our visits with our dad even decreased. I guess you can say we went from rarely seeing him to really rarely seeing him. And when we did, it usually was not an overnight visit.

My mom always tried to keep things positive in our house, especially when it came to our dad. She never let us say anything bad about him. Andy and I would get very frustrated when Dad would either forget to come and get us, or call and cancel. We would start to say negative things about him and Mom would remind us that he was still our father and that we should not say such things about him. I know deep down inside her, she wanted to join in on the "dad bashing," but she always tried to keep our feelings about our dad positive.

Needless to say, deep down inside Andy and I was a growing feeling of anger toward our father that would come to a head when we were older.

This was also the year that I first experienced death. My Opa died after a long bout with cancer. He was always the strong, silent type, but he was very good to Andy and me. He made Andy and me a bow and arrow, taught us how to find water for a well with the use of a baby apple tree branch, and showed us how to shoot a .22 caliber rifle. When Opa died, we were very sad. I can remember lying on my mom's bed as she told us about his death. I cried for a very long time. I did not know much about cancer or about death, so I was very lost and confused. Andy was also taking it hard, but somehow he stayed strong. He put his arm around me and told me that Opa was with God in heaven and that he would no longer be sick. Somehow, Andy understood death and the beauty of life. He told me to remember all the times we had with Opa and to think about them when I was sad. At the time, being ten years old, it didn't bring me much relief from my pain.

Several days after Opa's death, we had his funeral. When we entered the church, I did not want to go up for the viewing. Mom felt that it was important that Andy and I understand that this was part of life and that it was a way of paying respect to our Opa. I begrudgingly went up and saw my Opa lying in the coffin. I was horrified! I remember thinking that he looked different, lying there in the coffin, almost like a totally different person.

For several nights after the funeral, I had a recurring nightmare. I would dream the same dream each night. I would recreate the scene of my Opa's funeral, and when it was my turn to look into the casket, it was my dad's body inside the coffin. I would wake up screaming and crying, covered in sweat. After a while, the dreams stopped, but my memories of those dreams are still fresh in my mind. I was not sure what to make of the dream or why my dad was in the coffin, but I did know that I wished to be loved by my dad and I wanted us to have a great "father-son" relationship. Maybe my "wish" was actually just a dream itself, never to be a reality.

CHAPTER FIVE

Another new school year was approaching, and Mom would eventually pull Andy out of public school and put him in a Christian School called Chapel Christian Academy. He had flunked sixth grade while attending public school, but he was able to repeat it successfully at Chapel Christian Academy. Sixth grade was the first year that Andy had "failed," at least in his eyes and the eyes of the school. It was just a continuation of Andy not being able to express himself and the school being unable to find an effective way to get Andy to open up. But being strong enough to repeat sixth grade and complete it was a testament to Andy's ability to rebound from adversity and overcome his fear of failure. The hardest thing for Andy was knowing that he wasn't "stupid." The stutter and his fear of failure kept him from being able to prove that to his teachers and peers.

At about this time in his life is when Andy started to become an active member in the church. He was able to find solace and peace there. Now that Paul was studying to be a minister, we began attending his church. The members of the church did not treat Andy as if he was different and he began participating in youth groups and the choir. Andy always loved to sing. He had a deep baritone voice, even at an early age. He would sing along to tapes at home and never once would he stutter! It was baffling to me, and I remember being hard on him and telling him that if he could do it while singing, he could do it while speaking. Unfortunately for Andy, it was not as easy as it sounded.

Andy also found peace in reading from the Bible. I can remember as if it were yesterday, the clear and audible sounds of the scripture coming from his mouth as if God was speaking through him. Not a single stutter, stammer, or pause. I am still amazed by his ability to read scripture. I truly believe that the reason for this was both heavenly and earthly. I believe that God knew how hard Andy had to struggle every single day just to ask for a glass of water. I believe that he gave him the ability to read the Bible as his source of peace and to give him the confidence he needed to speak in his daily life. I also believe that a lot of Andy's stuttering problem was fear related. In church and in the privacy of our home, Andy could read the Bible without the fear of failure or being ridiculed.

Throughout seventh and eighth grade he maintained passing grades and was having some success in the classroom. Mom and Paul thought Andy was turning the corner. Success for Andy was not measured in the same way as it was for me or other kids his own age. To Andy, success was simply not failing. Andy would have highs and lows throughout the year, but if he ended up not failing, then the year was a success. Andy's seventh- and eighth-grade years were catered more toward his needs: smaller classes with more one-on-one interaction with the teachers. Unfortunately for all of us, ninth grade would not consist of small classes but large group lectures of twenty-five to thirty kids.

This is when Andy's fear of failure, the need to please my parents, and the desire to compete with my grades took control of his judgment. Every marking period in ninth grade was an adventure in our home. It was common for most schools, both public and private, to issue their report cards at about the same time every marking period.

That year, I was in seventh grade and every marking period, I would come home with straight A's on my report card. I sometimes wished that I had to struggle just a fraction of the amount that Andy did, just to show him that we were all human and that we all failed from time to time. But that was not the case, at least as far as school was concerned. I would show Mom and Paul my report card, and when Andy came home from school he would have no report card to show them. He would come up with some lie to tell my parents about the report card, figuring that if he didn't show it to them, they would just forget. That too was not the case. Ultimately, Andy would produce the report card, mostly consisting of D's and F's. Mom and Paul would be angry that he had lied, but they also recognized how hard it was for Andy to see those grades in print when he knew in his mind that he was smarter than the grades he received.

I knew Andy was as smart as I was. The reason I knew this was because I was his at home tutor. Even though I was a couple of grades behind him, I was able to understand his homework. I knew that Andy had trouble taking written exams. This wasn't because he had trouble reading or anything like that; it was just that the pressure would get to him and he would freeze. On a nightly basis, I would tape-record questions (true/false and multiple choice) that I got from his textbook. Andy would then take the practice test and he usually passed with a fairly high score. Unfortunately, he would go to school the next day and get all the questions wrong on the quiz or test. This was the perplexing thing about him; all that knowledge and no way to show that he knew the answers.

This trend continued throughout the year and he ultimately failed ninth grade. Andy was devastated and embarrassed. He really wished that he did not have to go through all the anguish a second time, having experienced it before when he failed sixth grade. But he knew that in order to succeed he had to go at it again. I remember sitting in our room and listening to Andy tell me how he wished he could get good grades. He also used to wish that school would just end and he could get a job and live a "normal" life. I would encourage him to continue to try hard and that I would help him graduate one day, even if he did so after I graduated. Andy promised me that he would never let himself graduate from high school after his little brother! Funny thing is I actually believed him too.

As if stuttering, having trouble learning, and having kids call you a "retard" was not enough for Andy, he had another problem that had surfaced in his life. Andy began having severe problems with his teeth. He had teeth growing out the roof of his mouth and sideways in his gums, and my parents became very concerned. They took him to the dentist, who recommended that Andy have several teeth pulled and that he would need braces. Add "tinsel teeth" to the list of names he was called!

Andy was very proud of his appearance. He liked to dress nicely, mostly wearing dress pants and a tie wherever he went. Having said this, knowing that he had teeth that were growing from places in his mouth that were abnormal sent him into a frenzy. Not only did Andy have to deal with his stutter, his grades, and his fears, he now had to survive the dreaded braces ordeal.

Andy was now turning into a man, at least physically. He was now sixteen years old, five foot nine inches tall, with a lanky build. His hair was dirty blond, but there was no discernable style to his hair. He wore it in a straight, even length and it basically just lay on his head like a well-groomed mop. He had mild acne, but no more than any other teenager did. He had a weathered look to his face, one that was brought on by years of stress and pain. However, he still had a glow, an aura, one that showed through all of his outward appearances. The only word that could effectively describe it is "hope."

Money was not in abundance in our house, so the expense of braces took a big bite out of our finances. But my parents always made sure that we had what we needed and they always found a way to get by in the end. Unfortunately for them, my actions at times made this a little tougher than it needed to be.

Not long after Andy got braces on his teeth, we had gotten into an argument. We were at home alone one day after school, and to this day I can't remember what we were arguing about. The thing I do remember about that day was that it was the first time that Andy ever got mad at me. If my memory is correct, I had done something to make Andy mad and he pushed me in the chest. I, in turn, punched him in the mouth, causing his mouth to bleed. I immediately felt bad for doing it and we went into the bathroom to see how bad his mouth was injured. Once we got into the bathroom and looked inside his mouth, Andy noticed that his inner lip and cheek were bleeding. Not only that, but I had broken one of the wires on his braces and it had cut into his cheek. This sent Andy into a fury! Without a stutter, he said, "You broke my new fucking braces, you asshole!"

Up until this time in my life, I had never seen Andy enraged like he was that day. I saw it in his eyes. I immediately ran away from him and he began to give chase. I made my way into the dining room and we began to play a game of cat and mouse around the table. I saw an opening through the living room and took it. I think this was the fastest I had ever run in my life! I made it into our bedroom and locked the door. Andy was pounding on the door, yelling at me to open up.

After a while, the banging and yelling stopped. I think two hours had passed since my escape into the bedroom. I assumed Andy had gone outside to play or was watching TV; either way I figured he had calmed down by this time. I slowly unlocked the door and opened it. BAM! Andy was waiting for me the whole time! He pounced on me like a cat on a mouse! I assumed the fetal position and he began to punch me in the head and back. By the time he was finished whooping my butt, I was sore and had a bloody nose. It was one of the rare times in our life together that Andy was the quintessential "big brother" and I was his submissive "little brother."

I never was really mad at him for beating me up. Actually, I was kind of happy he did. It showed me that no matter what I may have thought, he was still my big brother and that was not going to change! Moments like these, even though their magnitudes were not known at the time, were small steps toward Andy's independence.

CHAPTER SIX

The brightest spot in Andy's life during these difficult high school years was his "other life" at Camp Innabah, a Christian camp for kids and adults. He went to work there when Kristi told him they needed volunteer lawn keepers. Kristi was dating the camp director's son, Greg Troutman, at this time in Andy's life. Andy decided that it sounded like something he might enjoy. So, at the age of sixteen, off Andy went to Camp Innabah for a summer of cutting lawns, trimming hedges, and his first taste of teenage independence. Andy left home knowing that he had just finished a discouraging ninth-grade campaign, hoping that this new endeavor wasn't going to be a time for failure either. He lived on the campgrounds, did his own laundry, and found a niche for himself that would leave a legacy that he could never imagine.

The summer that Andy turned sixteen was the beginning of Andy's road to greatness. Andy began his new life at Camp Innabah. Almost immediately, Andy was welcomed with open arms by the staff and the campers. There was no need for a grace period where they had to figure Andy out. Those at Innabah had this unbelievable ability to accept all people, no matter how different they appeared. This was Andy's Garden of Eden, his utopia! Never before had he been accepted and liked by so many people. It was as if his stuttering and all his past struggles had never happened.

The entire first summer at Innabah, Andy was away from home. He came home occasionally for a good, home-cooked meal and because Mom and Paul really missed him terribly. Mom, however, did not want Andy to feel guilty about being away from home. She made sure that Andy knew that it was okay to be away and that she wanted him to experience life outside the confines of our home.

The first person Andy met at camp was the camp director, Gene Troutman. Gene knew of Andy's difficulties with his stuttering. Kristi took the time to explain to Gene who Andy was, prior to ever meeting him in person. Gene was a wonderful human being. His love for people and his strong foundation in the church helped to mold him into the man he was.

Gene did not treat Andy like someone who had special needs. He treated Andy with respect and never made him feel like he was any different from the other camp staff. Andy's job that summer was to mow the lawns and trim hedges. Andy and Gene were a perfect match as boss and employee: both were perfectionists. I recall Gene telling me on many occasions that he actually had to tell Andy to stop working when it was quitting time. However, Andy never wanted to leave a job undone and he usually convinced Gene to let him finish his work. Andy's workmate was an African-American gentleman named Otis. Otis was the first "real" friend Andy ever had, up to this point in his life. Otis was much older, but he accepted Andy for who he was and they formed this bond that would never be broken. Andy's favorite thing to do when he was not in school or working was to play basketball. This was what brought Andy and Otis together as friends. I can remember Andy coming home on one of his visits and all he could talk about was "Gene and I did this" or "Otis and I did that." I was beginning to think that someone else had taken my place in his life. I must admit, even though I had a lot of friends, I got rather used to Andy always wanting to hang around me. But eventually, I began to accept the fact that Andy was finally making friends and liking himself more and more every single day at Camp Innabah.

After a few days at the camp, other staff members began seeing Andy out on the basketball court shooting hoops. One by one, they all began to play with him. This became a ritual that most of the staff would do with Andy every day after work.

September was approaching fast, and that meant Andy had to return to school. If history were any gauge as to what this school year would be like, this year would again be a struggle for Andy. Up until this year, Andy had been enrolled at the Chapel Christian Academy. Having already failed ninth grade there, my mom was open to options as to where Andy should continue his education.

My grandmother Nan knew of a young man who graduated with my stepdad, Paul. His name was Matt Royer and he was starting a small Christian school called West-Mont Christian Academy that enrolled students from kindergarten through twelfth grade in the same building (total student population of a little over 100). Mr. Royer agreed to meet with Andy and my parents to see if a placement there would work. Andy was so nervous. Mr. Royer, seeing Andy's anxiety, asked Andy to play a game of basketball. Andy was "IN."

That year Andy began his new life at West-Mont Christian Academy. Andy entered ninth grade again, nervous but excited to have a new environment in which to learn. Andy arrived on the first day of school and Mr. Royer met him at the door. Somehow he knew that Andy needed a familiar face to greet him that first day at his new school.

Thus began what was to become the rebirth of Andy in a school environment. Somebody actually found the secret to unlocking the lid to Andy's "pitcher." Now, he still had struggles and by no means did he all of a sudden make the honor roll, but he was succeeding. And that to Andy was better than the honor roll on any given day! He had to take all the mandatory high school courses: English, science, math, history, etc. These were not special education classes. Even though Andy wished he had gotten straight A's like me, I was so proud of him for proving that he really could learn and that he was, in fact, SMART!

The great thing about this school, other than the fact that it was a new facility, was that a majority of the classes were video classes. The class was small in size and there was a faculty member there as a proctor. However, they used "virtual teachers" to teach the class. The proctor was there to answer any questions and monitor the students' work. This helped with Andy's confidence. He did not have to feel the pressure of an actual teacher standing over him and judging his every move. There was no desire to hide inside himself for fear of being called on in class to answer a question or go to speak in front of the class. No one to laugh at him, to snicker at or mimic his stuttering. He was finally comfortable.

He also started to make friends while at the school. The first student Andy really got to know and whom he secretly had a crush on was named Heather. She was a beautiful, smart brunette with a warm and friendly smile. The minute she met Andy, she befriended him. She was in his classes and always made it a point to sit next to him at lunch. I don't believe that she did this out of some form of pity, but rather a sincere desire to get to know him better.

I remember the day that class pictures were handed out to each student. Andy came home with a wallet-sized picture of Heather. On the back she wrote a little note that basically said he was very special to her and that she hoped they could continue to be friends for years to come. If you could have seen the smile on my brother's face that day after school. He was so happy to have that picture. He was so happy to have Heather as his friend.

I, of course, took this opportunity to tease him a bit. I kept asking him if she was his "girlfriend." He would reply, "Yes, she is a girl and she is my friend!" Not a bad comeback from Andy to his pesky little brother, although I think deep down inside him, he wished that she were in fact his "girlfriend" and not just a girl who was his friend. But this was not meant to be for Andy. Love would someday come his way, but not in the traditional sense of the word.

Left to right: Me and Andy, summer of 1980.

Me watching in awe of Andy's basketball-spinning abilities.
Christmas 1982.

Andy and I enjoying some "brotherly love" in the pool.
Summer 1983.

Andy, age sixteen, on his first day at Camp Innabah.

CHAPTER SEVEN

Thankfully, Andy made it through his second attempt at ninth grade. In June of that summer, Andy turned seventeen. We had a party at our house and Andy was asked who he wanted to invite to his party. He of course said the usual names: Kristi, Billy, Aunt Darlene, and our immediate family. However, one new name was on that list as well. He wanted Gene Troutman to be there. In Andy's heart, he felt that Gene was his source of comfort and strength. Gene happily came with his wife, Karen. One of my favorite pictures of my brother is from that day. It is a picture of Andy and Gene, arm in arm, with Andy smiling from ear to ear and giving the "thumbs-up" to the camera. That was how I remember him to this day.

With his newfound confidence in school, his second summer at Camp Innabah was sure to be a success. Andy arrived and saw some of the same faces he remembered from the prior summer. There were new faces there as well and Andy was excited to meet them.

Once again, Andy returned to his volunteer job in lawn maintenance. Andy continued to build his relationships with not only Gene and Otis but also the rest of the staff and the weekly influx of new campers. By this time, Andy was becoming a household name at Innabah. Campers who had spent time there the summer before were beginning to recognize him and some even asked for him when they arrived.

During Andy's second summer at Innabah, he began to spend more time with the camp counselors when his lawn work was done for the day. He would watch them with a curious desire to see what it was about them that the kids loved. Andy learned the camp songs, and to the surprise of most of the staff and campers, he did not stutter when he sang them. Gene observed Andy's interest in the counselors as well. Little did Andy know that Gene would have a big surprise for him the following summer.

Andy continued to grow both as a person and in his love for God. Being that this was a "church camp," praising God was a daily part of the camping experience. Every day they would have Bible class. They would also gather to sing hymns and talk about God. As Andy's confidence grew, he began to volunteer to read from the Bible in front of the staff and campers. This was a major accomplishment for Andy. A far as I know, he had never volunteered to read in public before. Once again the powers of God never cease to amaze me; Andy read each scripture with minimal stuttering. To many at the camp, this was nothing short of a miracle!

Gene and his family were Andy's surrogate family that summer. Andy did not come home as often, but we did make weekly trips to see him at the camp. Gene and his wife, Karen, routinely had Andy over for dinner. Gene even began to refer to Andy as one of his sons. This made Andy feel very wanted and special. He liked knowing that someone other than his family felt so strongly about him. It also was nice knowing that Kristi was there a lot too, since she was still dating their son, Greg.

Another successful summer at Camp Innabah was coming to an end. For the first time in Andy's life, I saw confidence in his eyes when he came home for good to start the school year. His fear was slowly subsiding. Andy was now in the tenth grade. With Andy's newfound inner strength, he began to be a little more assertive. West-Mont Christian Academy, being a new school, and a small one at that, did not have enough high school students to field any varsity sports teams. Instead, they conducted intramural sports.

Andy joined the soccer and basketball teams. To Andy's amazement, he quickly became one of the stars on both teams. His God-given speed and his ability to shoot a jump shot were unmatched by anyone on his team. This was the first time, outside of playing against me, that Andy was "the best."

I remember going to one of his soccer scrimmages to watch him play. I naturally assumed that Andy would play soccer the same way he did when we were little, as if he were lost! Boy did I get the surprise of my life. Andy was actually pretty darn good! He understood the basic rules of the game and he could kick the living tar out of the soccer ball. Andy scored a goal that game. I was so proud of him.

Tenth grade was not without its bumps in the road. Andy still had difficulties with his schoolwork and he still lied about his report card, but his grades were improved. He got B's in Bible class and gym, C's and D's in his core classes, and no F's. But Andy felt he should be getting better grades, and out of habit and fear, he continued to assume Mom and Paul were not going to be proud of his grades. It was the complete opposite: they were so proud of him. It wasn't until the last part of the school year that Andy figured this out.

Andy passed tenth grade. He was now eighteen years old. Being so old and only going into eleventh grade had Andy upset. He knew that the other kids in his class were only sixteen years old and he started to feel a little uncomfortable. Andy knew that most kids his age were graduating high school. Andy began to ponder whether or not he wanted to be what he believed he was: the only eighteen-year-old eleventh-grade student in the history of high school education.

He sat down with Mom and Paul and told them how he felt. My parents, knowing how hard he had struggled just to make it this far, told him that they would not be disappointed in him if he decided to drop out of school and get his GED. My parents only wanted what was best for Andy. Both of them knew that Andy was not going to be attending Yale anytime soon. They felt it might benefit him more to go out into the work force, since he was doing so well working at Camp Innabah. But in the back of Paul's mind, he knew that Andy should "finish the race." He urged my mom to encourage Andy to continue on with high school. She knew that Paul was right, but she also knew that Andy was emotionally and spiritually tired from all the years of pain and stress. She agreed to do the "right thing" and encouraged Andy to keep fighting and not to throw in the towel and give up on his high school diploma.

Andy then came to me for my advice. I reminded him of my promise to him: "I am going to help you graduate, even if it is after I graduate." Andy decided to go to Innabah for the summer and think about his future while working at the camp. Andy arrived at Innabah, assuming that he would return to his job on the lawn crew. Gene had another plan for him, though. Andy became an official "paid" summer employee. Up until now, Andy was only a volunteer employee. His only pay was his room and board. My parents had decided to pay him a small weekly stipend, but he had never in his life had an actual paycheck. Gene had another surprise for Andy that year. Andy was still assigned to the lawn crew, but his duties were being expanded. Andy was now a part-time counselor as well. Andy was floored! He never imagined that he would be allowed to be a counselor, what with having a stuttering problem and all the effort it took for him to express his thoughts to other people.

Andy had found his calling. He was now able to help kids. Throughout the summer, kids of all ages, races, and ethnicities came to the camp. Andy excelled in his new role, but the campers Andy really took a liking to were those with physical and mental disabilities. Most staffers would refer to them as "the kids with muscular dystrophy" or "the kids with Down's syndrome," etc. Andy, on the other hand, simply referred to them as the "special kids." Andy knew their pain. He had lived with similar stigmas attached to him his whole life. Andy made it a point to learn each of their names. He took an interest in their interests. He never treated them as if they were different. These kids LOVED him. And he LOVED them back. Andy would rush to get done his maintenance responsibilities, just to spend time with "his kids."

That summer, Andy got a nickname for the first time in his life. This was the first time Andy ever truly wanted to be called a name. Usually it was "retard," "weirdo," or something derogatory in nature. He finally got to be called a name that meant the people calling him it actually liked him! His new nickname was the "Birdman." The reason he got this nickname was due to the fact that he was so skinny that he had what is known as a bird chest. Andy didn't care why they called him the Birdman. He just liked it. Every new camper ended up knowing him as the Birdman or they simply called him "Bird."

Andy also decided that he needed a new hairstyle that summer as well. That summer the staff decided that he needed a buzz haircut. Otis, who had a completely shaved head, did the honors. I remember going to Innabah to see Andy that summer and the first time I saw his buzzed head, I cracked up laughing! Andy calmly informed me that it was a "cool" haircut and told me to shut up. Knowing that he really liked it, I controlled my laughter.

It had now been two summers at Camp Innabah and Andy was quickly becoming a celebrity there. However, Andy still had to decide what he wanted to do as far as his future in school was concerned. When Andy came home for good after the summer had ended, he announced that he was going to give school one more shot. This was the best news we, as a family, could have heard from him. Andy went into eleventh grade with a new outlook, knowing that he had to give it all he had to make it to the ultimate goal of graduation day.

Unfortunately, my own crisis was apparently going to overshadow the news that Andy was going to stay in school. As Andy made strides forward toward his goal of graduating high school, my life started to come unraveled a bit. I was able to keep up a decent faux front, but in reality my life was quickly starting to spiral out of control. Up until this year, I had always been a "leader," but for the first time in my life I became a "follower." Granted, I was always a "smart ass" and I started smoking cigarettes at thirteen years old, but I was basically a good kid who tried to always "do the right thing." This particular year, I was having a lot of emotional issues and found it hard to "do the right thing."

All the years of disappointment in my relationship with my father, my constant battles of will with my stepfather, and all the teenage pressures started to cause me to act out. I became more and more angry, especially at home. I felt like I was living a double life. School was fine, as far as my grades were concerned, but everything outside of school seemed to be going haywire. I started to hang out with the wrong crowd, committing minor criminal acts and getting away with them. I began to experiment with marijuana and occasionally drank alcohol. I liked the feeling of "freedom" that smoking, drinking, and all of those things gave me. Home, as far as it related to me, was very restrictive. Paul ran a tight ship with strict curfews and no foul language; basically controlling every aspect of my life.

Andy had his own demons to deal with, one's that were totally different from my own. My demons were mostly caused by my need to be "free." "Free" from the pain of my relationship with my dad, "free" from my perceived overly restrictive home life, "free" from all the teenage pressures. Most of the people that knew me, aside from my friends, thought I had the world firmly in my grasp. In reality, I had no idea who I was, where I was going, or what my future had to offer. I had so many mixed-up emotions stirring in my head that I could not focus. School came too easy for me and it required very little effort to do well. I was in the school band, but I really had no ambitions to be "the best" at that either. I played sports, but I was too busy working thirty hours a week to put too much effort into improving my hitting or foul-shooting skills. Basically, I just skated through life.

Mom and Paul knew I was acting differently and knew something was wrong, but they did not know the extent of my problems. I was starting to get migraine headaches, and as a result of those headaches I took a large quantity of aspirin. I also kept all of my feelings bottled up inside me. I refused to talk to my mom or Paul about how I was feeling. All the pent-up frustrations, emotions, and anger came to a head one morning in the spring, after Paul sent me to my room for being disrespectful to my mom.

I had failed to inform my parents that I had been bleeding rectally for over a week, and when I went to my room, I passed out. Mom came to the room a short while later and found me semi-unconscious on my bed. She rushed me to the doctor, who determined that I needed to be immediately admitted to the hospital to treat internal bleeding. At fifteen years old, I had a bleeding ulcer. I had been bleeding internally for a week and my red-cell count was near fatal. I spent that week in the hospital, getting blood transfusions and learning why I was in this predicament. It turned out to be a chain reaction that caused my ulcers. My headaches were being caused by stress, and the multitude of aspirin I ingested actually ate through the lining of my upper intestine, causing a rather large bleeding ulcer.

Once out of the hospital, my parents sat me down to discuss my life and what could possibly be causing all this stress. I could not talk to them. I was so angry, upset, and confused, and to be honest, I didn't like them too much at that time in my life. I agreed to seek counseling via the guidance counselor at my high school.

Mr. Baer, one of the school guidance counselors, agreed to meet with me twice a week to discuss whatever happened to be on my mind that day. I was initially very skeptical and did not trust his promise that our conversations would be strictly confidential. However, after a few sessions, I began to open up to him. I confided my innermost secrets, feelings, and aspirations to him. He proved to be trustworthy and actually seemed to be helping me cope with all my internal issues. Granted, a lot of my problems were not fixable, but he provided me with ways to deal with the way I reacted to stress on a daily basis.

Surprisingly, my parents respected my privacy, as far as my sessions with Mr. Baer were concerned. Certain aspects of my life improved and certain aspects did not. I continued to smoke cigarettes and occasionally smoked marijuana. I no longer drank alcohol, but that was more due to how easily it could be detected on my breath by my parents. I tried to disassociate myself from that "wrong crowd," but at times I found myself in precarious situations anyway. I did find ways to deal with my stress. I altered my diet, cutting out fried foods and the like, and continued to talk to Mr. Baer. My life started to become more stable; at least I was trying to make it so.

My desire for "freedom" came in the form of my job. I was a busboy/pizza cook at a local pizzeria. The employees there treated me like an adult. I immersed myself in work, usually working forty hours a week, for no other reason than to feel "free." I guess, looking back, I was only hiding from my life, but it seemed to be the right choice at the time. I was still a lost soul, hoping for some divine intervention to show me my way in life.

CHAPTER EIGHT

Andy arrived for his junior year in high school with a broad smile and an even bigger desire to prove all those who doubted him wrong. The great thing about West-Mont Christian Academy was the fact that all grades were in the same school. Since Andy was so fond of kids and he loved playing with them and helping them, this was a great place for him to be. Not only did he have a chance to befriend those in his class, he also befriended some of the younger students as well and he always made sure he said hi when he saw them in the halls. I am sure that when a fifth-grade kid gets a hello from an upperclassman, he is walking on cloud nine for the remainder of the day. I think Andy knew this and liked to make the younger kids happy.

Andy continued to do better in his core classes. Even though he had to struggle to make C's, eleventh grade was a year of great successes for Andy in the classroom. I could see a difference in him. There were times at night when I would quiz him about a subject he had a test on the next day. Andy would calmly answer all the questions with this uncharacteristic cockiness. As if to say, "C'mon, is that the best you got?" Never before did I witness Andy so ready to go take a test. The reason for all of this, I am convinced, was Camp Innabah and all the people he met there who accepted him for who he was. It allowed Andy the opportunity to grow in a pressure-free environment. Every year I saw his progression in high school and it always coincided with another great learning experience at Camp Innabah.

Andy and I seemed to be getting even closer during this particular year. We started to do things that teenage brothers would do together. He was actually beginning to act like my older brother. We went to my high school basketball games together and we hung out at the local Pizza Hut after football games. He got to know more of my friends and they accepted Andy. This was a major deal to my brother: being accepted by my friends. He always felt like he could never make his own friends, and he was especially jealous of my friendships as well. Finally, in his eyes, he was just like me. If he only knew, he was actually a better person than I ever could have been!

One of my most memorable moments with Andy actually involved the police! I was not immune to occasional police contact, but this occasion happened to be a rather humorous one. There was this one occasion where Andy and I were playing basketball at a local elementary school playground. Our basketball had gone flat and I made one of my many "boneheaded" decisions: I decided that I would climb onto the roof of the school and retrieve one of the many balls that undoubtedly had been kicked up there by some kid throughout the year.

The plan was for me to climb onto the roof and Andy was to act as the lookout for the cops. I found my way onto the roof and found a couple of basketballs to choose from. I threw them down to Andy and then decided that we might as well get the kick balls and tennis balls that were up there too! All of a sudden, Andy began to yell to me, but he was stuttering profusely. I didn't understand what he was trying to say at first, but once I stopped to listen, I heard it loud and clear: "M-M-M-M-M-M-MATT ... C-C-C-C-C-COPS!"

Unfortunately for us, by the time I got to the edge of the roof to see if Andy was right, it was too late! We were busted! The cop was standing there with my brother in one hand and the other hand was giving me that "come here, you little puke" wave that I had come to know so well! Even though I got Andy mixed up in my stupid plan, I did take the heat for it when the cop brought us home to Mom. Andy was actually pretty cool about the entire incident. The best part of the entire day was the fact that we got a new basketball that was full of air! I convinced the cop that the basketball that we owned was the one I got from on the roof. So even though we got punished for doing what we did, Andy and I got a new basketball out of it! That incident, no matter how stupid of an idea it was, was what being brothers was all about: being pals, covering for each other when one of us screwed up, and having secrets that no one else ever knew about. Those were the things that bound us together.

By this time in Andy's life, I was only a grade behind him in school. I was in tenth grade, playing in the high school band, playing baseball, and trying to gain the attention of many pretty girls at my school. One thing my school had that Andy's did not was a varsity basketball team. Andy loved to come to games and watch the team play. Andy's favorite player was a freshman named Del Savage. He was touted as the next great player to come out of our fabled basketball program. Our team routinely won the league championship, and the games were well attended by the students, faculty, and the community. Andy liked him not only because he could shoot a jump shot but also because he could dunk like no one he had ever seen before. Andy would always pester me during the games, wanting to know when Del would do another dunk. When that moment in the game occurred, Andy would stand up and go bananas! I have to admit it was a little embarrassing at times watching him scream and holler like a lunatic, but God forbid if anyone ever said anything mean to my brother about it in front of me! Andy was my brother and no one—I mean NO ONE—would ever get away with treating him badly! For all the problems I was having in my own messed-up life that was one constant that never would change.

Toward the end of the school year, Andy made my parents aware that he was ready to learn how to drive. He told them that since he was eighteen years old, he should be allowed to get his license. My mom was a little hesitant to allow him to drive, but Paul insisted that he could teach him and that all would be fine. Just before the school year was about to end, Paul began to teach Andy how to drive. This undertaking turned out to be one that Paul did not expect.

First, both our family vehicles had manual transmissions. Learning how to drive a "stick shift" is hard for any person, let alone my brother. Second, Andy was a perfectionist and hated to fail. This also threw a wrinkle into Paul's plans. It is very difficult to teach a person how to drive who has a desire to do everything perfectly and also who is deathly afraid to fail! Every day when they came home from driving practice, Andy would be upset and Paul would have that little vein on his left temple twitching! But, to both their credits, they stuck with it and finally, Andy was ready to take his driver's examination!

Andy was now nineteen years old and beginning to have the same wants and desires as most other nineteen-year-old kids. He wanted to drive, not only because he wanted to have a car, but also to feel "normal." Andy was not blind to the fact that most kids his age were either in college or out in the work force. He also knew that he was ready to take on this challenge!

It was a warm Saturday morning in early June when Andy got up at his usual 6 a.m. The driver's examination was at 9 a.m., but Andy liked to get up early on most days to "prepare" for whatever he had to do that day. Paul awoke around 7:30 a.m. and Andy already had eaten his breakfast, showered, shaved, and was basically waiting by the door to leave. Paul got himself ready and out the door they went. I had to work that morning at the pizza shop where I had been working since I was fourteen years old. I waited by the phone for the call telling me whether or not he had passed his test.

I got the call around noon. My mom was crying on the phone, which could have been either a good or a bad thing, since she cried for both! This occasion, however, was a happy one! Andy had passed his driver's test and did so without any infractions whatsoever. Andy, for once in his life, felt like he finally accomplished a goal! He basically got an A on his driver's examination. This was the first time in his life that he had ever done that well on any test he had taken!

The next thing on Andy's list of things to do was to buy a car. He and Paul spent weekends looking for the perfect car for Andy. Andy insisted on buying a car with a manual transmission; he liked the challenge! They finally found the car that Andy would fall in love with. It was a 1979 white Volkswagen Rabbit. It needed a paint job, but it ran great! Andy didn't have the money yet to get it painted, but he was so proud to finally have his own set of wheels!

That summer he arrived at Camp Innabah, not in the passenger seat of my parents' car, but in the driver's seat of HIS brand-new car! Everyone at the camp was so surprised and happy for him. Andy was so proud of himself that he could not contain his joy! He treated that car with the same care and perfection that he did everything else he owned. He was constantly washing it, cleaning out the inside, polishing the dash, and cleaning the windows. That car was his gold medal, his validation that all his struggles were worth it! He was "normal" in his own eyes for the first time in his life!

That whole summer, Andy walked around with a confident "strut." All the staff took notice that he had changed since the previous summer. Andy was a new man! Andy also began to experience the joys of a social life, a direct result of having his own wheels! He was now the man in demand. Those that did not have a way to the McDonald's soon found a willing driver in Andy. Any chance he had to drive his car he took! That summer at Innabah was probably the most memorable summer in Andy's life. He climbed his mountain of adversity and started to become a man.

During the late summer of that same year, I learned that my stepmother, Janet, was pregnant. I was not too happy about this, especially since I found out about it third-hand. My dad told me that he did not know how to tell me, fearing that I would not take the news well. Boy was he right! On the day I actually found out, I went over to my dad's house and an argument ensued. I went on a rant about how dare he mess up another defenseless kid's life and how dare he feel that he deserved a "second chance" with another child. I said some very ugly and hurtful words to Janet, and the result of those words was my dad punching me in the mouth and knocking me to the kitchen floor. He threw me out of the house and for several months, we did not speak.

Andy, as usual, was very happy for Dad and Janet. He continued to see them and went to their house frequently. Not that Dad or Janet ever seemed to care, but Andy was such an understanding and non-judgmental person that he would never have thought to say the things to them as I had. It just wasn't who he was.

Several months had passed and I began to forget about the big fight with my dad. We did not speak to one another, but I had the desire to reach out to him to try and patch up our relationship. In February of 1988, my dad and stepmother, Janet, had a little baby girl named Katherine. She was beautiful and definitely looked like a Cubbler. However, I was not completely at ease with the fact that my dad now had another child. Deep inside my soul, I guess I felt slighted. I doubt that Andy did, only because it wasn't in his nature. I, on the other hand, felt that it was one more person to compete with for my dad's affections. I was happy to finally have a sister and I in no way felt that she was to blame, but the facts were the facts … I had been trying for seventeen years to earn my dad's love and respect and this new situation did nothing to help me in that quest.

CHAPTER NINE

Once again, another summer at Camp Innabah was complete. Andy was so prepared to start his senior year in high school. To Andy, this was the last mile in the long and arduous marathon he called life. This is also the year Andy found the love of his life, Jane Marie Giaquinto. She was a sixteen-year-old girl who lived in a nearby town.

Now that Andy could drive, he took up a new hobby … bowling! Andy was a natural bowler. Andy joined a league at the local bowling alley. Even in the beginning of his bowling career, he bowled in the high 190s, which I am told is pretty darn good. Jane Marie was a bowler in this league as well. The day that they had met, she and Andy began to talk. The first words that came out of Andy's mouth epitomized the love he had for me and how proud he was that I was his brother. I am not sure I deserved such lofty respect, but it was genuine and I was proud to be his brother.

Most guys when they meet a girl try to impress them by making themselves look good; Andy, on the other hand, chose a different route. Andy's first words to Jane Marie were, "Do you want to see a picture of my brother, Matt?" So out of his wallet he pulls my school picture, and from that moment on, he and Jane Marie had a connection. I guess that was Andy's version of a "pick-up" line. Not one I would have used, mind you, but it seemed to work just fine for him!

Every Tuesday and Friday night, he and Jane Marie would meet at the bowling alley to bowl and talk. This led to phone calls at home, but the only place they would meet was the bowling alley. This was Andy's safety zone with his newfound love. Andy had to walk softly in this new area of his life. Never before had he cared for someone of the opposite sex, let alone have them care for him too.

Slowly but surely, their relationship continued to grow throughout the year. Luckily for Andy, Jane Marie was still young and not really ready for any type of serious relationship. So they were both content with the phone calls, bowling league, and the occasional chance encounter at the mall.

I never really asked Andy a lot of prying questions about his relationship with Jane Marie. He liked the fact that he had this special someone outside our home and that he didn't have to share her with anyone else. I let him have his space. The downside was that I never got to know how deeply Jane Marie really cared for him, until much later in my life. I assumed, wrongly of course, that Andy did not possess the ability to understand or maintain a relationship on this level. I guess I was just as guilty as everyone else was of short-changing Andy. I wish I had known better.

Our Nan and Pop were very loving and caring people to both Andy and me, but Andy had a special relationship with Nan. Even though we are not blood relatives, they are as close to our "blood" as any grandparents could be. Andy felt at ease when he went to Nan and Pop's house. Once Andy began driving, he spent a lot of time at their house. Nan loved him dearly, as did Pop. But Andy always loved to see Nan and talk to her. Yes, I said talk. Andy rarely ever stuttered in front of Nan. It was as if he never had the impediment. She would have an hour-long conversation with him. And on the rare occasion that he did begin to stutter, she had the ability to calm him down with her soft voice. I wish I could have bottled that ability she had so I could give it to all the families of stuttering children. She was amazing with Andy. As she would always say, Andy is my "special friend."

During his senior year, Andy continued to work at Camp Innabah on the weekends. Andy needed this to keep things in his life normal. He would still play basketball with the staff and help Otis lead songs at the campfires. Andy needed all of this to feel whole and part of a group that accepted him "just as he was." He also needed the money to help keep that car on the road too!

Andy also continued to build his relationship with Jane Marie. Things were finally starting to come together for him. He could see the finish line ahead of him. Nothing could derail his once-unattainable goal of graduating from high school. He spent the remainder of the school year completing the core classes he needed to graduate. He continued to play soccer and basketball on the school intramural teams. Basically, he was doing all the things that all normal high school seniors did.

In June of 1988, just days after Andy turned twenty years old he finally reached the finish line. He walked up onto that stage at West-Mont Christian Academy wearing a white cap and gown, shook the hand of Matt Royer, and calmly accepted his diploma. In his eyes, and the eyes of all those in attendance, he had finally made it. He accomplished something that no one ever felt that he would be able to accomplish. Not the psychologists from his childhood, not the administrators or teachers from his elementary and middle schools, not the bullies in the neighborhood who daily called him a retard— no one except Andy, our friends and family, and West-Mont Christian Academy believed in him. As he walked off that stage, he was holding a white rose, given to the students by the school staff. Andy walked over to Mom and leaned over and kissed her on the cheek. He handed her the rose and thanked her for helping him see his future and for not letting him give up.

Andy's first friend at West-Mont, Heather, was the class valedictorian. During her speech to the class, filled with promises of the future and what may lie in store for them down the road, she made one comment that stood out above the rest. She told everyone in attendance that she should not be the one up on stage speaking to the class. She stated that the one person who deserved to be on that stage was, "Andy Cubbler. No one worked harder to graduate than he did."

All the years of heartache and pain, all the struggles and tests, all the fear and shame were now gone. He was just like every other kid he thought was normal—a high school graduate!

Andy could hardly contain his joy. He was, for the first time in his entire life, proud of himself. He recognized the fact that he was able to accomplish a goal, one that was seemingly impossible when the journey began. No special education classes and no special treatment were given to him. He did it, albeit the hard way! He had "finished the race" and the "lid to his pitcher" was finally lifted and he could now go on in life with the confidence and knowledge that comes with success.

Andy shooting hoops in the driveway.

Left to right: Our maternal grandparents, Opa and Oma (Alfred and Herta Linnemeier).

Andy and I with our paternal grandparents, Pop-Pop and Mom-Mom (Roy and Mildred Cubbler).

Our parents, Paul and Mom.

Our step-grandparents, Nan and Pop
(George and Eleanor Jones).

CHAPTER TEN

No one knew that 1989 was going to be not only the year of Andy's greatest achievements but also the source of so much sadness.

After graduation, Andy began working at the Frederick Mennonite Home. He started off working the dayshift as a maintenance man. The home was a retirement community and also a nursing home for the elderly. Andy was always a good and hard worker. This, however, was the first job with salary and benefits that he ever had. He felt a great sense of freedom and independence that he never had felt before. His boss, Blake, loved him and so did the residents. Andy was always there to help those in need. Whether that aid was in the form of changing a light bulb for an old woman or helping up an old man who had fallen down, Andy was always there with a smile. Andy was given responsibilities and he took great pride in doing good work.

Andy was what I would describe as a little "anal-retentive" about the quality of work he produced. If Andy were tasked with buffing the hallway floors at the home and the shine on the wax floors was not up to his standards, he would stay past his shift until it was done right. I, on the other hand, was not nearly as concerned about such things. I was your normal eighteen-year-old boy; working was a necessity and I only did what was necessary and not one bit more! However, I did admire Andy's work ethic and his dedication to his job.

In the spring on 1989, I enlisted in the United States Army. I had the grades and the SAT scores to get into just about any college or university, but I was still very rebellious and I liked the idea of being out of the house, away from my restrictive life, and out in the world exploring. I chose a job in the intelligence field and had the choice of where I wanted to be stationed. I chose Germany ... far enough away and the land of my ancestors. Mom and Paul were less than pleased with my decision to enlist, but they came to the realization that it was MY choice. After a few months, they actually began warming up to the whole concept.

In June of 1989, I graduated from high school. Andy turned twenty-one and my stepdad took him out for his first legal beer. This was such a big day for Andy. No one, not even me, believed that he would ever graduate high school, get his driver's license, get a good job, or live the life of a "normal" twenty-one-year-old man. He did accomplish all these things, overcoming what looked like insurmountable odds.

Andy, however, was not immune from the occasional "screw-up." Although I was usually the one to get caught drinking or staying out past curfew, there was one—yes, only ONE—occasion where the heat was not on me in that department. One evening, after Andy's twenty-first birthday, he had met a few of the kids from his old school at the bowling alley. This place was Andy's place to not only bowl but also to socialize and talk to people he felt comfortable with. The kids he met there were about eighteen years old, but since Andy's school's enrollment was so small, he knew all the kids that went there.

As I stated earlier, Andy was growing into his own man, but he was still very naïve and he continued to struggle to make friends and to keep the ones he had already made. On this particular night, I came home from work at about 10:30 p.m. and my mom was sitting in the living room. She had a worried look on her face and I asked her what was wrong. She stated that Andy had told her that he would be home at 10 p.m. and it was now going on 11 p.m. To most people, this would not be considered something to be worried about. But for my mom, it was a major concern. Andy was not only "anal-retentive" about his work, he was also a stickler for being on time for everything, including when he would be home. Mom, knowing this trait in Andy, sensed that something was wrong.

She called the bowling alley, our grandmother, and all the local police departments and hospitals in the area and there was no sign of Andy. At about midnight, we saw headlights pull into the driveway. A few moments later, Andy came walking through the door. I was still up with Mom in the living room, trying to keep her calm. I must admit, however, that there was a part of me that was curious to see what kind of story Andy would have to keep himself out of trouble!

It was apparent when he walked in that something was not right about him. Mom immediately began to grill him about how he had her worried and why he did not call and so on. Andy stood there with a stoically blank look on his face. I thought to myself, "Man, does he have some set of balls or what!" I had to admit, I was impressed with his resiliency! What happened next was one for the record books. I wished we had a video camera at that time because it would have made a great scene in a movie someday!

Mom asked him where he had been and Andy replied that he was bowling with his friends. He then went on to tell her in an almost matter-of-fact tone that he had gone out drinking as well. Andy began to tell the story of the events of the evening, when I noticed that he was not stuttering at all and he was not even a bit nervous about the trouble he was facing with Mom. He told us how well he had bowled and that a few of the friends from his old school were there as well. He stated that they asked him to buy them a case of beer. Andy, being a little naïve, agreed to buy the beer. They gave him a six-pack, which I thought was a nice gesture by them to allow Andy to partake in their illegal adventure! Andy apparently drank about four or five beers, and when he looked at his watch he saw it was time to head home. Andy had made the drive home a hundred times from the bowling alley, but he had never done it with a good buzz on! According to Andy, he got on the highway in the wrong direction and by the time he realized that he was going the wrong way, he was about twenty miles from home! Somehow, he got his bearings together and finally made it to the house.

After hearing this, Mom went through the roof! She lectured him on the dangers of buying alcohol for underage kids and for driving drunk. And in between the parental lecture were a couple of lines such as "How stupid could you be?" and "What the hell were you thinking?" Ah ... I remember those lectures well! It was just nice to be a spectator in this one. I even made a couple of comments as well, just to seem like I was part of the conversation! However, this was not even the best part of the evening.

Earlier that same year, Mom had caught me smoking on the front porch. Having been a smoker once herself, she knew the hazards involved with smoking cigarettes. But this still did not stop her from making me smoke a whole pack in front of her as my punishment! She wanted me to get sick and throw up after it, but I just went out and bought another pack!

A similar tactic was used when Andy had come home drunk that night. Mom went to the refrigerator and came back with a six-pack of Busch Beer. She forced him to drink the whole six-pack in front of her. If it were I in Andy's situation, I probably would have puked after drinking the whole six-pack after the four or five beers he had earlier. Not my brother! He sat there unimpressed and asked her if he could go to bed. Mom, once again defeated at her own game, relented.

I followed Andy up the steps to our room and I asked him he felt okay after all those beers, and he told me, "I feel fine, just a little tired." He retreated to his room and went to sleep. The next morning, I woke up and Andy was already in the kitchen eating breakfast. I assumed he had a nasty hangover, but he informed me that he never felt better. People have called my brother many things, but a drinker was not one of them. But somehow he was able to survive his one and only bout with a good drunk with ease!

One part of both of our lives that was not getting any better with age was our relationship with our dad. Andy only wished that Dad would notice all of his accomplishments and show some interest in his life. Even though Dad did not show an interest in Andy, Andy showed an interest in him. Now that he could drive and had his own car, Andy liked to drive to Dad's house to see him. Every time Andy went over to see our dad, he came back a little sadder.

Dad had this knack for failing to put Andy's life into context. An attainable goal for me, such as college, was not one for Andy. Dad could not seem to accept that Andy was a little different and that to Andy, graduating high school and driving his own car to work were in themselves huge accomplishments.

The only thing our dad could muster, as far as interest in Andy's life, was his constant negativity about Andy and his "future." He always told Andy that working at Camp Innabah and Frederick Mennonite Home was not what he considered to be "career jobs." Andy did not look that far into the future. His struggles growing up and all his life entailed had taught him to take things one step at a time. Dad refused to accept this as reality. To Dad, Andy was a lost teenager who did not have direction in his life. But what is the saddest part is that Andy believed that he finally had direction and wanted so much for Dad to see that he was heading down a path of success and accomplishment.

I shied away from talking about my future when Andy was around, because I felt guilty. I knew it wasn't fair to have Andy compared to me or anyone else. But I was also struggling to gain my father's acceptance and his affection. I guess that no matter what the differences were in our present lives or our future ones, Andy and I really did not appear that much different in our father's eyes … a hindrance!

Dad seemed to be either blinded by what he wished in his own heart Andy would be, or he was just completely oblivious to who his firstborn actually was. Andy was everything every other loving father in the world could hope their son would become—a hard-working, kind, and loving person. Unfortunately, that would never be enough for our dad.

CHAPTER ELEVEN

Every year, our family would make the trek down to Rehoboth Beach, Delaware, for our annual vacation. In the beginning of July of 1989 our family went there once again. The plan was for all of us to stay down there for one week, and then my parents were to drive us back home. They were then going to return to Rehoboth Beach for a second week while Andy and I worked at our respective jobs. I was set to leave for the U.S. Army in August and this was to be our last official "family vacation."

Andy and I both took off a week from our respective jobs and we actually looked forward to a week of just hanging out on the beach and walking the boardwalk in the evening.

The first few days at the shore, Andy and I hung out together most of the day and night. On the third night, Andy and I were playing wiffle ball on the beach with a group of kids and I was also making an attempt to keep the kite I bought earlier that day aloft. Sitting on the side watching the game and also watching me struggle with the kite was this beautiful girl who just happened to catch my eye. She had long, brunette hair; deep, dark-brown eyes; and was thin and totally hot! I thought to myself that I had no chance of talking to her and that she was way out of my league!

But a funny thing happened that night. Andy began to have a conversation with her while I was up to bat in the waffle ball game. After I was finished batting, I went over to see what it was they could be talking about. Andy was struggling mightily with his stuttering. He was not nervous, I don't think, but it seemed like an eternity had gone by before he finished his first sentence. I quickly stepped in and began to finish his sentences for him, trying to alleviate any stress he may have been feeling about trying to talk without stuttering. Andy quickly reminded me that he was the older brother and did not need my help talking. Erin, the beautiful brunette, followed up Andy's remark with one of her own: "I think he is doing just fine here by himself!" Feeling a little outnumbered, I decided that the task of keeping my kite in the air was a little safer at that moment.

A short time elapsed and they both came over to where I was sitting. Andy introduced her to me and pointed out that I was his little brother. She was eighteen years old and so was I. Andy was twenty-one and I figured she was too young for him. So, being the hormonal teenager that I was, I decided to give her a taste of the "Cubbler Charm." In the beginning, it seemed to be backfiring. I kept trying to get Andy to leave us alone for a few minutes, hinting that he should be playing in the game and things like that.

Unfortunately, Andy was not the problem, Erin was. She could see right through my "Cubbler Charm" and knew exactly what it was I was trying to do. Finally, she said, "The only way you can talk to me is if Andy is part of the conversation." Not knowing if she was actually attracted to me or to my brother, I figured what the hell, she is very hot and as long as I am talking to her, I still have a chance with her!

She invited Andy and me to go out to get some pizza with her and her friends that evening. We all sat down in the pizza parlor and I made sure I sat next to her. She gave me a smile and then pulled out the seat on the other side of her for Andy. In my mind, I'm thinking, "What in the hell is going on here?" Andy was never a threat to me when it came to meeting girls. As far as I knew, the only relationship he ever had was with Jane Marie, and that was totally platonic in nature. I could not figure out what it was this girl saw in Andy. Usually girls that did not know him shied away due to his stuttering. Not Erin; she actually embraced his stuttering.

Once the pizza came and we all began to eat, Andy made a comment that to this day serves as one of the most hilarious and embarrassing moments of my life. I chose a slice of pepperoni pizza and devoured it! Andy, noticing my choice of toppings, blurted out without one ounce of stuttering, "Matt, you know pepperoni makes you fart! You better eat plain so you don't fart in front of everyone!" I turned about ten shades of red, but I laughed so hard that I could not eat! After that comment, I figured that Erin definitely would not want any part of seeing me anymore. But in a weird and cosmic sort of way, I think that Erin found my relationship with Andy to be something she found attractive in me. She saw our connection and knew that we were always there for one another, even when one of us outwardly tried to embarrass the other in public.

The rest of that week, Andy, Erin, and I were inseparable. We spent all day together on the beach and all night hanging out on the boardwalk. As the week came to an end, I realized that I was starting to have feelings for Erin. On our last night at Rehoboth, I convinced Andy to stay in so I could have one night alone with Erin. Andy was cool about it and he could tell how much I really liked her. I met her at her house and we took a long, slow walk on the beach together, holding hands and wishing we did not have to go home the next day. We sat on one of the lifeguard stands and I held her in my arms for a long while. I told her how much fun I had had and thanked her for being so nice to Andy. She looked into my eyes and thanked me for being such a good brother to him.

I was a little confused as to how, in five days or so, she was able to determine that I was a good brother. She said she could tell from the first time she met me. She stated that she knew when I was finishing his sentences when he was stuttering that I cared deeply about him. We sat there for a while longer, and I knew it was soon going to be time for us to say goodbye. We kissed and hugged and she promised to call when she got home to Maryland. She was the first girl I ever really cared about in a deep sort of way. Erin was a special girl.

One other memory I have of that week in Rehoboth was this corny family photo my parents decided we were going to do as a "family." It was one of those places where you get dressed up in the outfits from another era (Wild West, Civil War, etc.). They decided on the Civil War for our family photo. In retrospect, it was kind of fitting. Some nights in our house were like living in the Civil War, that's for sure! Neither Andy nor I was too happy at the time, which was evident by our long faces in the picture. We both felt like we were too old to be playing dress up. And neither of us wanted to take a family photo! Paul was a photography junkie, so family photos were commonplace in our house!

Up until this time, I was still pretty confused. I was still angry at the world, unsure of who I was or where I wanted to go. I enlisted in the army for all the wrong reasons. I really had no clue as to where my future was heading or what it was I was meant to become. The only thing I was sure of was that I needed to be on my own, free to do and act as I pleased. I assumed the army would provide me with that opportunity. College was not even on my mind. The last thing I felt I needed was to be forced to attend classes and do homework.

My relationship with my brother was one of my few constants. Although the roles in our relationship had begun to change, I knew I was always going to be my brother's keeper. Andy was now a man, no longer a boy who needed me to fight his battles. He could stand on his own two feet and meet all challenges head-on. That said, he knew he could count on me to be there, just in case he needed a little "backup."

CHAPTER TWELVE

When we arrived home from Rehoboth Beach, Andy and I went our separate ways. My parents returned to Rehoboth for another week to relax without the kids around. While our parents were away, Andy stayed with our grandparents (Nan and Pop) and I stayed with friends. Both were closer to our respective jobs and easier when it came time to eat dinner as well.

July 12, 1989, started off like most days. I got up, ate breakfast, and went to work at the pizza shop. Andy reported to work around 8 a.m. at the Mennonite Home. What happened next may seem like something from the *Twilight Zone*, but it is very much true. At about 4 p.m., I was in the pizza shop, when I suddenly felt the need to call Andy. I just felt something wasn't right and for whatever reason I felt the need to talk to him. The feeling I had was kind of like when someone comes up behind you and scares the hell out of you. I called Nan to see if he was home from work yet and she replied that he was not there. I can't explain why, but I was deathly worried about him. I usually did not worry, but for some reason I felt that something was wrong. I knew deep in my heart that he was in trouble, but I could not find a way to be certain. I had seen on TV how one twin sometimes can feel when the other twin is hurt or in trouble; now I know how they must have felt. I continued my shift at work, hoping Andy would turn up fine at Nan's for dinner.

At around 7:15 p.m. another eerie feeling came over my body. The only way to describe it is that I felt a part of me die. It was fear, horror, and panic all wrapped up in one. I felt as if a boulder had landed squarely on my chest. I ran from the kitchen and I yelled at the employee who was on the phone to get off, and quickly called my grandmother again. Again, I asked if Andy had made it there for diner. She once again stated that he never showed up and that she too was becoming very worried. I began to panic. I hung up and started to pace.

A few minutes later, I got a call from my dad at the pizza shop. His voice was crackling from trying to hold back tears. He informed me that Andy had been in a terrible auto accident on his way home from work. He said that he was in surgery and did not know if he was going to make it. I told him to call Mom and Paul at the beach, and he told me that he did and that they were on their way home as we spoke. I hung up the phone in a state of shock. I told my boss what had happened and he sent me home for the night. I went to the friend's house where I was staying and waited to hear from my mom. At about 10 p.m. that night, I got a call from my mom. She was crying hysterically and I told her that I had heard about the accident. I told her that I was staying at my friend's house for the night and that I would talk to her in the morning. I told her that I was too upset to drive.

Unfortunately for both my mom and me, she was calling to tell me that Andy had died! I did not realize this and when she heard me say that I knew about the accident, she was assuming that I knew he had died as well!

I spent the night praying to God to keep Andy with us on Earth and not to take him to heaven. The next morning I reported to work for the breakfast shift. A short while later, my mom walked through the front doors of the restaurant. She looked at me as she walked in the door as if I had three heads! I asked her how Andy was and she began to cry.

She asked me why I would come to work instead of coming home. I told her that there was nothing I could do at the hospital and that I was trying to keep my mind off of the accident by working. She the said to me five words that will remain in my head for eternity: "You mean you don't know?" With that, I began to panic. She proceeded to tell me that Andy had died in surgery and that he was gone forever! The next twenty-four hours were a complete blur! I remember going completely crazy inside the restaurant, throwing things and cursing God. After that, it becomes pretty fuzzy.

The next few days were spent preparing for Andy's funeral. I spent that time being very angry with everyone. I was mad at God for not hearing my prayers to spare Andy's life. I was mad at my parents, my biological father, the droves of people who kept coming by and rekindling the need to cry with my mom, but mostly I was very mad at myself for not being there to save him. That was my job. I was Andy's defender ever since we were kids. I hated myself for not being able to do ANYTHING to help him and for not being at the hospital on the night of the accident. This feeling would stay with me for many years after Andy's death.

Inside my head, all I could think about was Andy and my failures. I believed that I was somehow at fault for his death. I wanted to die. I was supposed to always be there for him, no matter what. I spent the next few days thinking about my life and whether I was the one who actually deserved to die. Luckily, it never actually came to me attempting suicide, but I definitely gave it some serious thought. I knew that Andy would not have wanted me to live the rest of my life that way and I knew he did not want me to kill myself over what amounted to a freak accident.

The funeral was a very difficult day for all of us. But there was something completely beautiful that occurred that day. You see, Andy never felt like he belonged. He had very few friends that I knew of. He was never "cool" and never "popular," as most kids strive to be when they are young. But for those of you who feel that those things are important in the grand scheme of things, you should have been at Andy's funeral. Andy may not have possessed any of those "desired" traits, but the ones he did have in great quantity were love, honesty, and trust.

Not only was every seat in the church full, there were about 150 more people outside who wanted to pay their respects to Andy. I never knew the magnitude of the life he lived. Who knew that so many people would be touched by his warmth and kindness? All those people were there for MY brother! As they poured into the church to say their goodbyes, I realized how truly beautiful Andy really was. These people, all there to show their love for Andy, knew him. They were touched by his life and they mourned his passing. The relationships that Andy had with all of these people were unique to each and every person who came to say goodbye.

Paul, being the minister at our church, had to preside over the funeral for his own son. I was still routinely at odds with Paul, being a loud-mouthed eighteen-year-old kid, but I look back on that day now with admiration and respect. I cannot imagine how difficult that had to have been for him that day. I am sure Andy was looking down on him from heaven, giving him the strength he needed to be strong for all of us.

Prior to leaving for the gravesite, I asked the funeral director if I could have a moment alone with Andy. I got into the back of the hearse and opened the casket. I was unable to look at Andy. I did not want that image to be the one that I remembered for the rest of my life. I asked the funeral director to point out at which end his head was located and I in turn looked at his feet instead. I reached up to the middle of the coffin and found his hand. I touched his hand, and I began to cry. I removed my high school class ring from my suit coat pocket and put it in his hand. I took his class ring from my coat pocket and placed it on my finger. I told him that I loved him and that I would never let go of his memory, and I asked him to forgive me for not being able to save him. I slowly exited the hearse and the funeral director closed the coffin.

At the burial site, all the people from Camp Innabah gathered around his gravesite. In unison, they began to sing

Andy's favorite camp songs. A choir of angels could not have sounded more heavenly! After the ceremony ended, I just sat by myself and cried. It was the only thing I could do at that time. After the funeral, all the staff from Camp Innabah returned to the campgrounds. They, without hesitation, went to the old, broken macadam basketball court with the bent and rusted rim that Andy loved to play on. They grabbed a basketball and began to play one last game of hoops in honor of Andy. There were lots of tears, stories of Andy, and some laughs as well as they paid tribute to their friend and my brother. Andy's work on Earth was done, but his "light" would continue to shine in the hearts of everyone who knew him.

Andy and Gene Troutman at
Andy's seventeenth birthday party.

Me and Andy, Christmas 1987.

Nan and Andy, her "special friend." Circa 1988.

Andy showing off his class ring on the eve of his high school graduation, June 1988.

"Civil War" portrait taken in Rehoboth Beach, Delaware. This was the last picture taken of our family, one week before Andy died.

CHAPTER THIRTEEN

The next few days were filled with a lot of pain, sadness, and reflection. I decided to talk to a counselor about my feelings of guilt. I was not ready to talk to anyone who knew Andy, since I was not ready to share my feelings on that level with someone I was close to. I needed a nonpartisan opinion. I needed someone who would not judge me and who would listen to my rants. I believe that this decision to talk to a counselor actually had saved my life in some respects. I walked away feeling better about myself. I also found some perspective with regard to my relationship with Andy and my relationship with my family. I had a clearer vision as to where I was headed and what I wanted to become. But I still had some unfinished business to take care of with Andy and his death.

As part of my need to come to grips with the loss of my brother, I decided that I needed to see his wrecked car. I am not sure why this was so important, but I needed to see it. I went to the junkyard that now owned Andy's prized VW Rabbit. As I walked to the rear of the yard, I began to feel sick to my stomach. I began to tremble and could not control my emotions. Andy's car was in the last row and against a chain-link fence. The entire front end of his car was completely smashed in. The roof was peeled away; this is the only way the rescuers were able to get to him. The force from the head-on impact caused the steering wheel to be pushed straight up into the roof of the car.

Earlier in the week, the police officer that investigated the accident advised our family that Andy was at fault in the accident. This was difficult to hear. Andy had never caused anyone harm before in his life, and to hear that he was "at fault" in anything was tough to hear. We asked the officer for information about the accident. He stated that based on the evidence and witness statements, it appeared that Andy was unconscious prior to hitting an oncoming vehicle head-on in the oncoming lane of traffic. The driver of the vehicle that Andy hit was much luckier than Andy was; he sustained only minor injuries in the accident. This was something for which we as a family were thankful. We did not want the burden of knowing that another person had died in the accident as well.

To this day, it is not known what happened to Andy on that dreadful day. My parents considered requesting the results of the autopsy to identify the cause of Andy's unexplainable unconsciousness, but the feeling in our family was, "What would this knowledge change?" Andy was still gone and this information would not bring him back to us. We also decided that Andy had suffered enough in his life and in his death. Knowing would not give us closure; it would only create a new place to experience pain. Pain was something that we had no more room for in our family.

A few days after the funeral, Nan was at the house to spend time with my mom and Paul to help them cope with the loss. She spoke to Mom about a feeling she had about Andy that would later come to be. In her heart, she believed that Andy would metaphorically return as a butterfly. To Nan, butterflies are peaceful, beautiful, and calming. It was her way of saying that Andy would always be here to keep an eye on us, and that when we needed something tangible to hold on to, look for a butterfly to calm our spirits. Maybe she was on to something.

About two weeks after Andy's accident, I had a little scare of my own to deal with. I was driving back from the local YMCA and crashed my car into the back of a school bus. Luckily, no one was injured in the accident and there were no children on the bus at the time of the accident. I sat in my car thinking to myself, "Why me?" I had no idea how to explain this to my parents. Calling my parents was not as easy as it would have been had my brother not just been killed in an accident.

I called and told my mom what had happened. I expected her to be upset, but what I did not expect was about to happen. My parents refused to pick me up at the scene. They were so angry with me! As my luck would have it (usually bad luck), my accident coincided with an appointment my parents had with the coroner's office to officially retrieve Andy's personal belongings.

So, in their place, they sent Nan and Pop to come and get me. I thought this was a blessing, since they were normally pretty cool about things. Boy was I wrong! Nan and Pop picked me up at the auto body shop that towed the car. Pop helped me remove all my belongings from the car and put them in his car. Nan sat in the car quietly, but she looked furious! Pop gave me some words of advice: "Just get in the car and don't say a word. Nan is not very happy with you!"

For the life of me, I could not understand why everyone was so mad at me. It was as if they thought I had done this on purpose! Like I chose to wreck my car and risk the chance of dying like my brother! I knew that they would be mad, since Andy had just died, but I thought they would then feel relieved that I was okay. Once gain, I assumed wrong!

Nan and Pop took me to their house. Nan refused to talk to me the whole way home. We went into the house and Nan told me to sit down at the kitchen table. She sternly asked if I was hungry. I told her I was a little, but not to go out of her way to cook me anything. Well, she definitely went out of her way. Ten minutes later, there were six pieces of tomato pie sitting in front of me. In Philadelphia, tomato pie is basically

Sicilian pizza without the cheese, eaten at room temperature. She instructed me that I had to eat every last piece of the pie and that when I was finished, she had dishes for me to wash.

An hour had passed and I finally struggled to get the last bite of tomato pie down my throat. I looked in the sink and saw only a few dishes to wash. I thought that I was going to get away with washing only a few dishes. Once again, I was wrong! Nan walked in to the kitchen and proceeded to empty all the silverware from the drawer into the sink. She instructed me to wash them thoroughly and then dry each piece. She stated that she would be in to inspect them when I was done drying them. So I begrudgingly washed all the dishes and silverware in the sink. I then dried everything and called for Nan to inspect my work. She found moisture in between the tines of a fork and proceeded to dump them all back into the sink. The only words that came out of her mouth were, "Do 'em again!"

With that, I mumbled something that loosely translated into how I thought she was being unfair. Wrong choice of words on my part! Nan then went into what is now affectionately known as the "Allegiance Speech." Nan tore into me about how I needed to show more allegiance to my family and how I was acting selfish and ungrateful.

I was either still in shock from my accident or just completely not interested in what she was saying, but I had no idea what she was talking about! I definitely had no idea how I went from wrecking my car to this! Needless to say, I sat there and took the verbal ripping from Nan and happily dried the dishes to her satisfaction. Thankfully for me, once I was done with the dishes, she gave me my opportunity to get out of her sight and sent me out to "the shop" with Pop.

"The shop" was a room in the back of the garage where my Pop did all his work. He was a locksmith, a carpenter, and he also had a tool-sharpening business. It was also the place where Andy and I could hang out and bond with Pop. It was a safe haven and I desperately needed a place like that on a day like this!

I gladly obliged and immediately went out to the shop to see Pop. Pop began to smile when I walked in and he asked me if Nan was still mad. I told him that she was and told him about the "Allegiance Speech" I had just received. He gave me a wry smile and a shoulder shrug, as if to say, "Yeah, I've been there myself!" That was the great thing about Pop; he could always relate to me. We were very much alike when he was my age!

He did, however, comfort me by confirming what I already knew: that I did not wreck my car on purpose. He told me to bite my tongue and to let them be mad for a while. Mom and Paul came to pick me up a short while later. I was once again summoned into the house to talk about the accident. Mom and Paul were still very angry. I tried to explain to them that I did not do this on purpose, but they wanted to yell instead of talk.

After listening to them rant about how I was being self-centered and not thinking about other people, I had finally had enough. I began to yell back. I told them that I was sad and mad about Andy dying too! I told them that no matter what they thought, it was an accident and that I could not control accidents! I decided that walking out of the house would definitely show them that I was serious, so out the door I went!

A minute or so later, Mom came out crying and gave me a hug. She apologized for the way everyone was treating me. She was just so scared and she was still feeling the emotional toll of Andy's death. She did not have enough emotional strength left inside her to deal with my accident! It was an unpleasant day, for sure, but I think some emotional healing occurred that day as well! As far as my "Allegiance Speech," Nan still refuses to clarify what she meant. Now she uses it as a threat against me if I am acting out of line or if I am in need of an attitude adjustment! Trust me; I've received my fair share of those speeches over the years!

The "Allegiance speech" is now a running joke during the holidays in our house. Every year I ask her, "What the hell did you mean by that anyway?"

She usually replies with, "Matthew ... if you don't get it by now, you never will!"

CHAPTER FOURTEEN

Life after Andy died was very difficult. A little over a month after his death, I began my enlistment in the United States Army. As a result of Andy's death, I had the opportunity to back out of my obligation to the army, but I chose to honor my commitment. I knew in my heart that Andy would have wanted it this way. He was so proud of me when I told him that I had enlisted in the army. He told me that he wanted me to be a hero.

I also knew that staying at home meant that there would be the constant reminder of Andy's death. I would see it in my family's eyes; in the hearts of friends and neighbors stopping by; and in his bedroom, which had been left untouched and in the same perfect way he left it every single day before he left for work. I didn't think that my soul could handle the pain and sorrow I felt when I sat in my bedroom at night, waiting to hear him say one more time, "G'nite Matt ... I love you!" So I chose to leave home to begin my new journey.

This was, as it turned out, the start of my version of "life goes on." This was my new course in life. I needed this to heal and I needed this to make sense of Andy's tragic death. I needed it to prove to myself that I did have a greater purpose in life. It was my way of validating everything that he was to me and to ensure that I lived up to his lofty expectations of me.

I left on August 29, 1989, for basic training at Fort Leonard Wood, Missouri. After Andy's death I felt the need to wear his high school class ring every day. It in some way was a tangible connection to him that I did not want to lose. The first week in the U.S. Army is spent at what is referred to as the reception station. Here you get issued your gear and learn a few basic rules that will help along the way. It is also very laid-back. I thought to myself, "This army stuff is pretty cool." Unfortunately, the army has a sick sense of humor, and they set it up this way so they can really shock the ever-loving crap out of you when you actually arrive at basic training!

On the day we were to report to our barracks for basic training, they loaded us into what is known as a "cattle truck." It is called this because at one time, they actually hauled cattle inside these trucks. I had one full duffel bag strapped to the front and one on my back as well. I also had my personal bag, containing my clothes from home, in my hand to top things off. We were then crammed into the cattle truck and we were ordered not to remove our duffel bags; we had to hold them during to trip over to the barracks. Once we arrived, a drill sergeant came onto the truck and began to scream at us, "Get the hell off of my cattle truck, you goddamned pieces of shit!" Ah … that's the army I had heard so much about!

Once off the truck, we had a whole slew of drill sergeants barking out orders to anyone who would listen. It was complete chaos! One yelling to go here, another yelling to go there, and somewhere under all the yelling was MY drill sergeant!

My drill sergeant was a "gentleman" (and I use that term loosely) named Staff Sergeant Cruz, from Guam. He was about five feet tall and built like a pit bull. I quickly realized after he began to yell at us the minute we got off the bus that he spoke with a heavy accent. I noticed that the only clearly understandable words that came spewing out of his mouth were curse words!

Once off the bus, we had to empty our duffel bags of our newly issued camouflage fatigues, black combat boots, and other U.S. Army-issued gear to make sure we were issued all that we would need for the next four years of our lives! After that was accomplished, we had to empty our personal bags with our civilian gear and personal items. Once those items were inventoried, we were ordered to place the items back into our personal bags to be turned in until we graduated from basic training. This included all unauthorized jewelry, except for those who were married and wore a wedding ring.

I stood in formation in complete shock. In my mind, I was not strong enough to handle all the probable stressful situations I was about to encounter in the army without Andy's ring securely on my finger. However, SSG Cruz was rather adamant about his desire to strip me of my source of strength and comfort. Not even a week into my U.S. Army career and I was faced with a decision: submit to their request or stand my ground. I chose to stand my ground.

I respectfully denied SSG Cruz his request for the ring. What I did not immediately realize were the repercussions of my blatant disregard of a direct order. I had just met this man and I was already disobeying an order. What the hell was I thinking? I quickly learned what it was like to have a five-foot-tall man scream at you while a steady stream of spit coated my face! On top of that, he felt that I needed to become one with the ground—via the now-infamous "grass drills."

At the time, I had no clue as to what a "grass drill" entailed, but I was quickly schooled in the art. First I was told to get into the push-up position, and I did push-ups until SSG Cruz was tired, then onto my back for "flutter kicks." I once again performed this drill until SSG Cruz was good and tired. The final drill was to run in place until my legs felt like wet noodles. I continued to repeat these drills for what seemed like an hour.

SSG Cruz once again asked me to relinquish Andy's ring to him and he assured me that I would have it back once I graduated from basic training. I once again advised him of the reasons that I could not allow the ring to leave my finger. Yep, you guessed it: more "grass drills!" This went on for quite some time, and after a while, I think we both came to realize that either I was going to die from exhaustion or SSG Cruz was going to lose his voice from screaming at me.

I was ordered into the office of Captain Smith, who was the company commander of my unit. Once inside, a host of intimidating men in uniform surrounded me. SSG Cruz, Captain Smith, and several other drill sergeants that I had not yet had the pleasure of meeting were all present. I must admit, though, that things were a lot less stressful in his office. He spoke to me like a normal person and we spoke candidly about Andy's recent death, my decision to honor my military commitment, and my desire to be in the army. I emphasized that I would not, under any circumstances, relinquish Andy's ring to them. I explained how I placed my class ring inside Andy's casket at the burial and how I promised him that I would wear it.

After a long discussion and a closed-door meeting between the captain and the drill sergeants, we were able to come to an agreement on the ring issue. I agreed to wear the ring on my dog tag chain and they agreed to stop torturing me for refusing to give it to them in the first place. Afterward, SSG Cruz came up to me and took me aside for a private conversation. I began to have flashbacks of the "grass drills" and I could still taste his spit on my lips. I was so afraid he was going to tell me to "sleep with both eyes open." This guy was a freak of nature and I would not want to meet him in a dark alley. I was truly glad he was in my army and not the enemy's!

However, to my surprise and relief, he actually complimented me on my ability to withstand extreme pain, all the while refusing to give in to their demands. He told me that was what the U.S. Army looks for in their soldiers … honor, dignity, and the will to fight against all odds.

After that conversation with SSG Cruz, I had a renewed sense of pride. I found strength, not only in the ring, but also inside my own soul. I knew that I could now face whatever obstacle came my way. Nothing could keep me from reaching my goals and making Andy proud.

During my time at basic training, I found myself feeling very alone. I missed Andy; it had only been a couple of months since his death. I tried to find a way to put my emotions into context. I needed to release the pain from my heart. I could not talk to anyone, since they were basically strangers to me. They could not begin to understand the magnitude of my pain.

One evening, I decided to write down my thoughts. I decided that a poem might help me heal. I had never really written a poem before and I was not sure how or where to begin. I decided that I would let the words flow from my mind, to my hands, and onto the paper and see where I ended up. The following is the first draft of that poem. It captured my innermost thoughts and I decided that it needed no editing or revision:

"Bro"

Some days are harder than others,
But the memories are still the same;
Anger and guilt usurp my mind.

Not a day goes by that I don't think of him;
Sometimes I laugh ... sometimes I cry.

I feel responsible
Yet I am not,
But still the pain remains.

A bond never to be broken—
Friendship beyond life ...

Things left unsaid,
But we knew somehow
We'd be closer in the end.

I'd die for him,
But he gave me new life.

I felt his pain,
His fears,
As if my own …

I knew the end had come …
Death left a message in my heart.

I hated the world.
I hated myself.
I loved him.

The healing never really comes,
But life does go on.

A final token of love,
Rings, molded to our hands:
An everlasting tie.

As reality sets in,
I cry.

Thank you, Brother,
For giving me
The true meaning of life!

I sent the poem to my mom, knowing that she might need it to help her through these dark days. I called about a week after sending the poem home and spoke to Mom. She had received the poem and I could tell that she was moved by the words and by the feelings with which it was written. I told her to keep it somewhere safe so it could be read by anyone who needed to know what it felt like to lose a son or a brother. I pray that no one else ever has to feel that pain.

CHAPTER FIFTEEN

In 1990, while stationed in Augsburg, Germany, I was given orders to deploy to the Middle East for the first Persian Gulf War. I found out shortly before Christmas of 1990 and promptly called Mom to tell her the news. Needless to say, she was sad and afraid for my safety. She did not want to risk losing her only surviving son to a war in a far-off land. I assured her that I would not be killed and that everything would be fine. I told her that Andy would keep a watchful eye on his little brother to keep me out of harm's way.

A few days before Christmas, I called Mom again to see how she was doing. She began to tell me about her most recent visit to the nursing home to see Oma. Oma had suffered a stroke earlier in the year and was suffering from bouts of dementia.

Mom proceeded to tell me that when she walked into Oma's room, she seemed to be very clear in her head and even knew the date and some current events. Oma then said something to Mom that was both eerily haunting and strangely soothing all at the same time. She said that Andy came to visit her earlier that day. Mom, knowing her mental state, replied, "No, Mom, Andy died. He couldn't have been here today." Oma kept insisting that she had indeed received a visit from Andy and that she knew that he had died. Mom, now curious, asked about the visit.

Oma began to tell Mom in full detail about the visit from Andy. She went on to explain that Andy had stopped by her room carrying a suitcase. She asked him where he was going and he replied, "I am going with Matt to the war." This startled Mom, since she had not yet told Oma that I was going to the war. She asked her how she knew I was going to the war and she replied, "Andy told me." She said that Andy had told her that "Matt needs me there to protect him," and that it was his job to do so.

Needless to say, I was overcome with emotions after my mom told me this story. I truly believed that Andy would be there in some fashion when I arrived in Saudi Arabia for the war.

In February of 1991, I arrived with a small contingent from my military intelligence unit in Dhahran, Saudi Arabia. The first day that we spent there was full of chaos and confusion. None of us actually knew what our role was to be while there. There were rumors flying around that we might me going to the front lines to give intelligence support to the armored units, and there were other rumors that had us in the rear, coordinating all war-related intelligence for the U.S. Army.

As we sat "homeless" on the tarmac, hundreds of U.S. and coalition aircraft were taking off overhead. I sat there wondering what it was that they would encounter once they reached their target. I also prayed that each and every one of them returned safely from their mission.

The following day, we received word that we would be temporarily assigned to our "sister" unit in Riyadh, Saudi Arabia. We took a six-hour bus ride from hell with a driver we affectionately called "Frank." He was a local, but he could not drive to save his life! We arrived in Riyadh, but no one really seemed to care. Our "sister" unit did not want anything to do with us and we ended up having to fend for ourselves when it came to food and water. We were given a place to sleep, but when it is 110 degrees, sleep is nonexistent.

As the day turned into night, I made my way to my sleeping quarters. I dropped the duffel bags from my shoulders, laid my M-16 rifle down next to them, and sat on my cot ... I was completely exhausted! The next thing that occurred bordered on either delusional or miraculous. I am not an expert on the indigenous insects of Saudi Arabia, but I am pretty sure that butterflies are not common in that part of the world. However, flying right before my eyes was none other than a black and yellow butterfly!

It was the most beautiful sight to behold. All I could do was stare at it as it fluttered about the room. It seemed to have a calming effect on my soul. I remembered Nan telling Mom that she believed that Andy would return to us in the form of a butterfly. I know it sounds hard to believe, and if it had not happened to me I'd be skeptical myself, but it is true. From that day forward, I felt calm, and confident that nothing bad was going to happen to me while I was involved in the Gulf War.

To Andy's credit, he did a great job of protecting his little brother! After four months in the sweltering 110-degree heat of the Middle East and what turned out to be a rather short war, as far as wars go anyway, I returned to my unit it Augsburg, Germany, to finish out my hitch in the army.

In 1991, my mom-Mom and Oma died, one just a few weeks apart from the other. Oma was a good, strong woman and a loving grandmother to both Andy and me. I believe that her final gift to us was her vision of Andy just before I left for the war. Both Mom and I will be forever in debt to her for that gift.

The news of Mom-Mom's death hit me very hard. I was still stationed in Germany and could not be there for her funeral. I came home a month or so later, hoping to get a few mementos from her estate to remember her by. Most of the estate was given to my dad and my uncle Roy. However, throughout her life she secretly gave important pieces of her life to my mom. Even though my mom and dad had been divorced for close to twenty years, my Mom-Mom continued to love my mom as if she were her own daughter.

One of the items she gave my mom was this gaudy, extremely large diamond ring. It had a large number of diamonds of different shapes and sizes, and she told Mom that she wanted her to have the ring and to use the diamonds as she wanted.

Mom-Mom knew that after she died, my mom and I would not be included in the disposition of her earthly belongings. She routinely would say that to me, anticipating the future. My dad and Uncle Roy never saw eye to eye on much, and after Mom-Mom's death that was even more apparent.

My dad and stepmother took what they thought was rightfully theirs after she died. Uncle Roy tried to be the good son and keep the peace in the family; but it appeared that my dad and stepmother wanted nothing to do with him, only what they could take from Mom-Mom's house. This was just another sad example of the man I spent most of my life trying to please.

In July 1993, I completed my enlistment in the U.S. Army. I got hired as a police officer soon after I got out of the army. In July of 1994, while working as a police officer, another phenomenal thing happened to me that I luckily lived to tell about.

While working the 3 p.m. to 11 p.m. shift in the borough of Royersford, Pennsylvania, a category F3 tornado tore through the town and the neighboring township of Limerick. I was on patrol on the main street of the town, checking for downed wires as a result of a heavy rainstorm. I noticed that the rain was beginning to stop. I continued my patrol with the windshield wipers off.

All of a sudden, a flood of water hit my car windshield. I feverishly tried to slow down my vehicle and I turned on the wipers to allow me to see where I was going. I felt a tree branch hit the side of my police cruiser and I still could not see out of the vehicle due to the amount of rain coming down.

I stopped the vehicle and decided that it was too dangerous to continue to drive under those conditions. I could faintly see the signs for Fifth Avenue and Main Street out the side window of the car.

What happened next was either divine intervention or unbelievable luck. I felt the car move, but I assumed it was the wind blowing against the side of the car. A few seconds later, I realized that it was not the wind … the car came slamming down to the ground! I sat there completely stunned. I gathered my senses and exited my police cruiser. The rain was now a light drizzle and the winds were beginning to calm down. I looked to see where I was, and to my surprise, I was now in the middle of the 700 block of Main Street, facing the opposite direction … two blocks away from where I had stopped the car!

I then turned to the car to see how I could have gone two full blocks without even noticing and I quickly realized that I had not gotten there by driving, that's for sure! All four tires were flat and the undercarriage of the car was crushed. In essence, the car was totaled!

I looked around and saw downed trees, overturned cars, and roofs blown off of houses. Then it hit me: I was just carried two whole blocks by a tornado. Needless to say, shock was an understatement. I am lucky to be alive to write about it.

Unfortunately, a family in Limerick, Pennsylvania, who happened to be sleeping peacefully in their house when the tornado hit that town, was not so lucky. A mother, father, and their baby girl perished. I won't begin to boast that I was one of the lucky ones chosen by God to survive that fateful night, but I do believe that Andy had a hand in the outcome.

Throughout my career in law enforcement, I encountered many potentially life-threatening situations. Some of those I lived through due to my knowledge and ability, but in some of those situations, I believe I had my guardian angel, Andy, watching over me. It is ironic how life works out. For all of our years together on Earth, I was "my brother's keeper." Now, after his death, Andy has taken on that role with me.

CHAPTER SIXTEEN

In November of 1994, I met the girl of my dreams. I was out at a bar with a childhood friend named Jeff Mickletz; it was just before Thanksgiving Day. We had a few drinks and listened to the band that was playing that night.

Lauren and her friend Michelle were there as well. Lauren was a beautiful blonde with an infectious smile. I remember giving her my business card with my pager number written on the back and I told her to page me if she wanted to go out on a date. She looked at the card and asked, "So you are a cop?"

I replied very confidently, "Yes, I am." Mind you, I can remember feeling that I was pretty cool back then.

I stood there in front of her, with a slight smirk and the thought racing through my mind, "Chicks definitely dig cops!"

She then looked at me with that infectious smile and stated, "Am I supposed to be impressed?" I was quickly brought back to Earth with my super male ego firmly in check.

However, three days later, she paged me and the rest, I can honestly say, is history. I finally found someone to share my life with, share my dreams with, and someone to create new dreams with as well. She was beautiful, smart, caring, and she liked ME! What else could I have asked for in a woman? Our first year of dating was magical and new. We learned everything we could about each other and we also found out what could make the other person angry. However, we also found out that making up was the best part of an argument! She was the one, I was sure of it!

Things in my life were going as I had hoped; I was working as a cop, I had met the girl of my dreams, and I was ready to make her my wife as soon as possible. However, life knocked on the proverbial door once again in the form of cancer.

In 1995, my mom was diagnosed with breast cancer. For most of her life, Mom has had to battle an assortment of health problems, but none as serious as this. The last thing any of us needed was the dreaded "C" word … CANCER! Needless to say, it brought back a lot of the pain of losing Andy and we now were fearful of her possible death as a result of the cancer.

However, Mom proved to be the ultimate soldier and she faced her fears and battled the mighty cancer. She underwent heavy doses of radiation and chemotherapy. She battled the nausea and fatigue. She fought tooth and nail to defeat this dreaded disease. After all the pain and suffering, her oncologists gave her a clean bill of health. They gave her hope that the cancer was completely eradicated from her body. However, as with all cancer patients, the five-year mark for remission is the "gold standard" when it comes to officially being "cancer free." We waited patiently for that day to come.

In May of 1996, I left the Royersford Police Department to pursue another police job in a department closer to my home in Pottstown, Pennsylvania. Even though she would not readily admit it, Lauren did like that fact that I was a cop. She liked the fact that I was trying to "save the world" one person at a time. She knew that I loved being a cop and she loved me for it.

Finally, in August of 1996, I asked her to be my wife. Prior to asking her to marry me, we had discussed the type of ring she might want if I decided to ask her to marry me. My mom, always the sentimental one, offered diamonds from the gaudy diamond ring that Mom-Mom had given to her before she had died. Lauren loved that idea and my plan was now to figure out how to ask her to marry me and how to create the perfect engagement ring out of the donated diamonds.

After asking for and receiving permission from her father to propose to her, I began trying to figure out how I was going to ask her to marry me. I initially wanted to do something creative and original to "pop" the question to Lauren. I hinted around to her about taking a hot-air-balloon ride and she advised that she had no interest in doing that. Boy was she making this tough!

I decided that I was going to freeze the ring in an ice cube and put it in a glass of water for her. The idea was for her to see the ring as she drank from the glass. Unfortunately, she was sick the day I was planning to ask her to marry me. I fixed her a glass of water with the engagement ring in one of the ice cubes. As my luck would have it, she was too sick to even drink the water, and as I stared at the glass, I could see the ice cube melting. The one with the ring inside of it finally melted and I could see the ring slowly sinking to the bottom of the glass. I quickly removed the glass from her view and removed the ring from the bottom of the glass.

I waited two more days, until Lauren was feeling better. She was over at my house and I decided that rather than taking the risk of her not seeing the ring in the ice cube or having it melt in the glass, I would ask her to make me a glass of water with the ice cubes in the freezer. I made sure that there was only one tray of cubes and that the engagement ring was inside one of those cubes. I patiently waited in the family room while she went to the kitchen to get my glass of water. From the kitchen I heard her ask me, "What is in the ice cube tray?" I played dumb and I told her to look closer at the item and to see if she could make out the shape. She studied it for a second and then she stated, "It looks like a bug."

I went into the kitchen, removed the cube from the tray, and carefully melted it under warm water. As the ice cube melted, she finally realized that it was not a bug, but in fact a diamond ring! I dried the ring off, got down on one knee and looked into her eyes, and asked her to marry me. She, of course, said yes!

The next few weeks were fantastic for Lauren and me. She was the one I was meant to spend my life with and I am sure the one that Andy would have approved of as well. She radiated happiness and that happiness was shared by me and both of our families. She could not wait to tell everyone she knew, and even some she didn't, that we were engaged.

I can remember sitting with her and just looking at her while she watched TV or read a book. She was so beautiful and she loved me, even with all the baggage I had been carrying around for so many years. She knew all about my life; the good, the bad, and the ugly. She accepted me and my faults and supported me when I needed a shoulder to lean on. She knew about Andy and how his death changed me, and she helped to keep my head on straight when I sometimes veered off course. She even knew all about my tenuous relationship with my dad.

Even as an adult, I was still trying to win over my dad. I still felt as if he was waiting for me to accomplish some unknown goal, one only he had knowledge of. I kept thinking that I might get lucky and prove my worth to him. Then I would see the love and respect emanate from his eyes. Unfortunately, life has a way of running its course and some things are just not meant to be.

My soon-to-be mother-in-law advised us that she was going to call the newspaper and submit our engagement announcement. She asked me how I wanted my portion worded in the announcement. I advised her that I wanted it written as follows: "Matthew Cubbler, son of Rev. Paul and Louise Jones." The announcement appeared in the newspaper's Sunday edition the following week. At the time, I chose to have it worded in that way because I felt that Paul had earned the right to be listed as my parent. My poor relationship with my dad and his lack of interest in both my and Andy's lives made me feel as if he had not earned that privilege of being named in print as my parent. This decision was one that I would have to live with for the rest of my life.

I received a call from my stepmother, Janet, shortly after the engagement announcement appeared in the newspaper. She left a message on my answering machine, berating me and calling me a horrible son for not including them in the announcement. I immediately called back and tried to explain to her why I made the decision to omit their names in the engagement announcement. She hung up on me. I called back and asked to speak to my father. He got on the line and he spoke in a very calm and monotone voice. He spoke as if he had rehearsed his words. He told me that he was hurt and I told him that I felt that he had not earned the right to be hurt.

He then went on to tell me that my nine-year-old half sister, Katherine, was also very hurt by my actions. He told me that she felt slighted because she was not asked to be a flower girl in our wedding. I told my dad that we already had two flower girls and that I never once spoke to Katherine about becoming a flower girl. I accused him of putting thoughts into her head. I also had a feeling that Janet had something to do with it as well.

I asked to speak to Katherine. She too sounded very calm on the phone and was speaking to me as if she was reading from a piece of paper. She told me that she was upset about not being a flower girl and that she did not want to come to the wedding. I asked her if she felt that way or if Dad or Janet told her to say that. She replied that she was sad, but she was told to say she was not coming to the wedding.

My dad quickly took the phone from her and told me that I was a horrible son and brother. I told him that if Katherine did not want to come to the wedding that he should force her to come since she is only nine years old. He told me that she would not be attending and that was final. I finally put my foot down and told my dad that if Katherine was not going to attend, neither were they!

The next few words that came out of my father's mouth still haunt me to this day. He replied by telling me that I was dead in his eyes! I responded with, "Dad, I have been dead in your eyes since the day I was born and so was Andy!" The phone line went dead and those were the last words I ever spoke to my dad.

I cried, not only due to the finality of the moment, but also for the twenty-five years of emotional pain that I had endured at the hands of my father. This was not the way I envisioned my relationship with him ending. I envisioned us finally finding some type of common ground to build a relationship upon. I envisioned heartfelt apologies, hugs, and forgiveness. That, I guess, was not how it was meant to be. I always wanted to have some sort of closure, but never in a million years did I expect it to end like that. I could not believe what had just happened; the end of my tumultuous relationship with my father, eradicated from his memory forever, as if I never existed in the first place.

I picked up the pieces of my shattered heart and dusted myself off. I decided that Lauren and our future were too important for me to be sad and depressed. I decided to put my father and the pain behind me, at least for the immediate future.

So, on May 3, 1997, Lauren Marie Cording became Lauren Marie Cubbler, my wife. Our wedding was a glorious affair at on old plantation-style mansion that had since been turned into a restaurant/banquet facility. We had 150 friends and family in attendance and we danced and socialized throughout the evening.

My best man in the wedding was Kevin Gilroy. Kevin was part of the family I stayed with frequently in high school and I also went to his place the night of Andy's accident. The Gilroy family was a second family to me. They "adopted" me as one of their own and that act of love and kindness helped me tremendously while dealing with my brother's death.

Due to Andy's death, I became an only child. I needed to have siblings in my life and the Gilroys definitely filled that need. Kevin was one of the few friends in my life who truly understood Andy, and he was the one I chose to be my best man due to his kinship with Andy. Kevin's twin brother, Chris, was also a groomsman, and he too understood Andy. Not only had the Gilroys accepted me into their family, but they accepted Andy as well. For this I am truly grateful.

My best friend, Brian Skelton, a police officer with whom I worked, was also in my wedding party. Brian and I became instant friends when I got hired as a police officer. Brian is one of those fun-loving guys who are always willing to go on a road trip at the drop of a hat to the casinos in Atlantic City. He is also someone you can call and talk to any time, usually about absolutely nothing of any real importance. He is a true friend in every sense of the word. There is nothing he or I would not do for one another. We shared many experiences on and off duty, and his personality and loyalty made him an easy choice to be a groomsman in the wedding.

The final member of my wedding party was my best friend from my U.S. Army days, Jamie Hall. Jamie and I became friends while stationed in Augsburg, Germany. Jamie was a good old country boy from Kentucky. He was half Cherokee and he had a deep Southern drawl. However, if you ask any of the women who attended the wedding, it was his amazing good looks that set him apart from all the other men in attendance … including me! Jamie was always the guy who could attract the ladies. However, for me, he was a true and loyal friend. There was never a time where he did not "have my back" in any situation. He would walk to hell and back for me and that was all I needed to be just as loyal to him. He was a natural choice to be my final groomsman.

The reason this was so important to me was that Andy should have and would have been my best man. In the days leading up to the wedding, I questioned myself and I questioned if Andy would approve of the men I had chosen to represent my life on my wedding day. I thought about all the things that Andy was to me: a brother, a friend, a confidant, and the one and only guy who I knew throughout our life together definitely "had my back."

I looked over my choices of groomsmen and they definitely had all the qualities that Andy had while he was alive. That knowledge put my mind and soul at ease and convinced me that my choices were solid ones.

As I stood proudly with my new bride in front of our friends and family, I am sure Andy was standing right there next to me, with his hand on my shoulder. I am sure he was giving me a gentle squeeze, just to show that he was happy and at peace with my decision to marry Lauren. Then I am sure he looked down the row of groomsmen and gave them a big "thumbs-up" as a sign of his approval.

CHAPTER SEVENTEEN

It was a new chapter in my life, one that now included my beautiful wife, Lauren. We were now a family. We looked forward to the future and what it might bring, but we also took the time to savor the present, knowing how lucky we were to have finally found our "soul mate."

Lauren and I moved into the house that I had bought about a year before the wedding. It was a small, brick Duplex in Pottstown, Pennsylvania. It was an old house, but it was ours and that was all we really cared about.

This was also the year that Gene Troutman, Andy's boss at Camp Innabah, began to put into motion the dream he had envisioned since Andy's death. His vision was to raise enough money through donations and fundraisers to build a facility that would include a gymnasium, recreation center, and rooms where everyone could gather and share God's love. His motivation was Andy. He loved him so much in life and missed him even more since his death. He wanted to honor Andy's life, and the impact he had on so many people, by naming the gymnasium "Andy's Court." The first of many fundraisers was held early in the year and the first dollar was raised to bring that dream closer to reality.

My family was touched and honored that Gene and Camp Innabah had thought so highly of Andy. We, as a family, never would have expected that anyone would pay such an amazing honor to Andy. Gene's vision and motivation and the charitable contributions of so many people made us all believe that Andy's Court could actually come true. Gene placed his entire heart and soul into this project and our only hope was that we would one day be standing, united in the spirit of love and peace, in the center of the gymnasium honoring Andy's Court.

After the news of Andy's Court, I felt a renewed sense of purpose. It gave me a clearer vision as to what I wanted in my life. Part of that vision was my desire to start a family with Lauren. I knew I wanted to have children at some point in time, and prior to our wedding, Lauren and I spoke often about starting a family soon after we were married. We wasted very little time getting started!

In June of 1997, one month after our wedding, Lauren bought a home pregnancy test. After a few minutes in the bathroom, she came out with the biggest smile on her face. As you can probably guess, it was positive! She was carrying our child and that news was more than my heart could take. I was so happy, but I was also a little sad that Andy was not around to be the first one I called with the good news.

The next few months were spent by me getting the new nursery ready, and for Lauren, attending numerous baby showers. We decided that we wanted to know the sex of our unborn child. Neither Lauren nor I were too hip on surprises and we wanted to have the room and the accessories ready for the baby's birth. At her five-month exam at her OB/GYN, an ultrasound test was performed. The baby was not cooperating too well that day, but the doctor was 99 percent sure that we were going to be having a baby girl. We were both very happy with the news. Not that we were hoping for one sex in particular, but a little girl sounded so great right at that moment.

On February 16, 1998, Lauren's father had called to inform me that Lauren was on her way to the hospital from her work. He told me that Lauren's water had broken and that we were going to have a baby soon. The only problem with this news was that Lauren was not due until March 23. I quickly rushed to the hospital to be with my wife. After speaking with the doctors, it was determined that they were going to keep Lauren in the hospital and monitor the baby's vital statistics.

February 16 came and went. No baby! February 17 came and went. Still no baby! By this time, Lauren was exhausted and so was I. She was getting pain medication through an IV tube in her arm, but the contractions were getting worse. It was a very long labor and the pain, the contractions, and the sheer exhaustion were starting to take their toll on her.

However, early in morning on February 18, the labor reached its all-time high. The doctor's advised that the baby was soon to arrive and they began to prepare for the birth of our soon-to-be baby girl. Finally at 5:32 a.m., little Rebecca Cubbler was born! She was six-weeks premature, weighed five pounds twelve ounces, and was nineteen inches long. She was absolutely the most beautiful baby I had ever seen, not that I was prejudiced or anything!

We decided to give her a unique middle name in honor of my German heritage and my brother. We gave her the middle name of Linne, short for Linnemeier, which was Andy's middle name and my mother's maiden name. When I told my mom about our decision, believe me, I made sure she knew how thoughtful I was not to have burdened little Rebecca with "Linnemeier" as her middle name! Needless to say, I got a loving smack on the arm from Mom for that comment!

After a few days in the hospital, Lauren and Becca—as we liked to call her—came home from the hospital. The first few months at home with a new baby were tough for Lauren and me. Having a baby and having no clue how to be good parents made each day an adventure. We asked our parents for guidance, but ultimately, we were going to have to "wing it" on our own. We both came from loving, solid families. Our instincts and our faith in God helped us in making those first and most important parental decisions.

Every decision, whether it was how often to change her diaper or when to feed her, was made on the fly. Lauren tried breast-feeding for two months, but she could not produce enough milk to sustain Becca's constant desire to eat. It also was taking a huge toll on Lauren's health as well. She never got more than two consecutive hours of sleep and she was having trouble dealing with all the other responsibilities that came with being a mother. I was working rotating shifts at the police department and I was only of limited use in the feeding area! We finally decided to switch Becca to formula. Lauren was so relieved to finally get four or five consecutive hours of sleep!

Lauren was also going to graduate school part-time during her pregnancy and after Becca was born. Lauren had graduated summa cumme laude from Drexel University in Philadelphia in 1995. She received her bachelor's degree in marketing, but quickly realized that she wanted to be a teacher. She graduated with her teaching degree in elementary education in 1998 and was hired full-time as a kindergarten teacher in a public school near our home in 1999. She loved teaching and she was very good at it as well. She had found her "calling" and it made Lauren and our family very proud to see her so happy and comfortable with her new profession.

Throughout the pregnancy and the first year with Becca in our lives, I looked to Andy for guidance. Even though he never had kids, or a steady girlfriend for that matter, I somehow knew he would guide Lauren and me down the right path.

A couple of years had now passed; we were finally getting the hang of being parents. Becca was a beautiful little girl. She was bright, loving, and the spitting image of her beautiful mother! We read her lots of books, looked at photo albums, and identified all the people in the pictures.

When we got to pictures of Andy, I tried to explain to her, in a way that she would understand, who her uncle Andy was and why he was not here. I explained to her that he was my brother and that he was up in heaven, looking down on her every day. I told her how her middle name was given to her in honor of him. I wanted her to have as many early memories of Andy as possible. I didn't want his picture or his identity to be foreign to her.

Another way in which I tried to integrate Andy into her life was by referring to Andy through symbolization. An example of this was the way I comforted Becca during a bad thunderstorm. On stormy nights, when there was a lot of thunder and lightning, I would tell her that she never had to be afraid of the loud, booming thunder. I explained to her that the thunder was just Uncle Andy and God playing a friendly game of bowling.

I did not want her uncle Andy to be just a picture she could find on a wall or in a photo album. I wanted her to be able to have something tangible that she could understand. Using a thunderstorm as the catalyst to help her think about Andy served two purposes: it kept Andy and his spirit in her heart and mind, and it also served to make thunderstorms less frightening.

Lauren was getting more and more accustomed to my hectic work schedule, and Becca liked the fact that her daddy was a police officer. She always liked when I would come home from work on my dinner break. I made a special effort to turn on the emergency lights for her when I left the house. Daddy was her personal superhero; at least I liked to think that way!

As I continued to work as a police officer, I found myself always trying to find a new challenge. I loved the idea that the public "needed" me to keep them safe at night or to help them when they were in trouble. There is a saying among cops: "We face what you fear!" I believed that I was put on this Earth to help people, no matter what dangers might lurk around the corner. I was never satisfied with the standard approach or the safe approach. If there was a child being abused, I found a way to save him or her from the abuser. If there was a vehicle accident scene where a person was trapped, I found a way to get the person out and to a safe place. If there was a burning building with people trapped inside, I ran in without hesitation.

In 1996, I decided to join the SWAT (Special Weapons and Tactics) team. As the years went by, I worked and trained even harder to perfect this specialty and I was promoted to team Leader in 2000.

SWAT is called to a scene when the patrol officers inform the "higher-ups" that the situation requires a more specialized response. We had special equipment and more training than the average street-level police officer did. We were called out for service for a variety of situations: high-risk search warrants, barricaded gunmen, hostage rescue, and bomb-threat/terrorism situations.

I was always one of the first officers through the door on any given SWAT call out. I sometimes wondered why I put myself in harm's way. I never really gave it much thought while I was actually doing it. That usually came after the fact. Deep down inside me, I think I might have been trying to correct past childhood mistakes. Another thought was that I might have subconsciously been trying to make up for not being able to save Andy. I don't know.

Part of me also thinks that it might just be who I am as a person. I believe that after Andy died, my course in life changed for a specific reason. I was not sure where it was heading specifically, but I knew that I was good at my job and that I had a knack for being in the right place at the right time to help people. I believe that everyone is put on this Earth to accomplish something great. Whether that is a big or small accomplishment, only God knows the answer to that question. As for me, I had to rely on my faith to keep my compass pointed straight ahead, taking each step as God, and I am sure Andy, had laid it out before me.

CHAPTER EIGHTEEN

Just when you think things are going as planned, life has a way of throwing you a high fastball, right under your chin.

Fear! Panic! Doubt! The year 2000, or "Y2K" as it was called, caused a lot of people to experience some, if not all, of those emotions. However, on January 1, 2000, people awoke from their slumber to find that the world was the same as it had been the day before. The millennium came and went with a whisper. All the hype over Y2K was just that ... hype! All the end-of-the-world conspiracy theorists spent the first day of the new millennium wishing they hadn't spent $3,000 on a generator that could power a small city! All the makers of "Duct Tape" and bottled water were laughing all the way to their local banks. Needless to say, it was a very uneventful start to a much-anticipated year.

For me personally, Y2K was a year of change. I was not prepared for the highs and lows that this year would offer, and on some levels I wished it never had come at all. In the spring of 2000, Aunt Darlene, my surrogate parent for so many years, died of a rare neurological disease called Progressive Supranuclear Palsy (PSP). It is a very ugly and ferocious disease.

Medical experts have no cure for it and only approximately 10,000 people are known to have had this disease. The only well-known person to have suffered and died from this disease was the actor Dudley Moore. Some medical experts have referred to the disease as Parkinson's disease's ugly cousin.

Kristi and Greg took her into their home to care for her and to assure her that she would not be alone in her fight against this ugly disease. They exhausted all of their financial resources, all of their energy, and all of their time to ensure her comfort. Not a day went by that Aunt Darlene did not have loved ones by her side. Kristi loved her mom and she knew that she needed to be strong for her, just like Aunt Darlene was strong for all of us when we were kids. It was the least we, as a family, could do for her, and I thank Kristi and Greg for the compassion and love they showed her during her finals days on this Earth. I am sure that she and Andy are sitting on a beach chair, on a scenic beach, somewhere in heaven, just like the days when the "Mighty Moms" took all us kids to Rehoboth Beach.

Aunt Darlene was a fantastic woman who gave of herself without any strings attached and with only the purest intentions. She loved unconditionally and was as much a mother to me as my own mother was. She helped to mold Andy and me into the men we had become and instilled values, morals, and love into our hearts.

She suffered for a few years with PSP, but she never stopped fighting, not until her very last breath. She could not walk, could not talk, and could not use her arms to give a hug when we came to visit her. However, when you looked into her eyes, you could see that her mind was still working 100 percent. She still could feel, she still could cry, and she still could love, unconditionally and without hesitation. I loved her back, unconditionally and without hesitation. She will be sorely missed.

Once I started to come to grips with the loss of Aunt Darlene, I tried to focus on my life and my career. The new millennium served as a catalyst for me professionally. I was still motivated to catch the bad guys, but I was beginning to feel lost. I was becoming disenfranchised over how the legal system worked. I was tired of arresting someone and seeing that same person back on the street corner the next night. I was tired of seeing death and poverty. Basically, I was burning out. I new I needed a change, but I had no idea what that change could be. I loved my profession, but I needed something to give me a "jump start," a change of scenery maybe, a new challenge.

Lauren and I were starting to feel cramped in our house in Pottstown. We began looking around in neighboring communities for a new place to live. We found a new development that we really liked and we picked out a house that we loved and could afford. Construction began in October of 2000 and we moved into our new four-bedroom, two-and-a-half-bath home with a big yard in January of 2001. It was not only the first new house for Lauren and me, but it was also the first new house that I had ever lived in ... EVER!

In August of 2001, Lauren began her third year of teaching, feeling more and more confident in her abilities and loving the opportunity to be part of the education of America's youth. Becca was growing up so fast and becoming quite the personality. She was becoming a little lady who loved to read stories, play with her dolls, and sing songs.

I was so proud of Lauren and her ability to juggle a full-time job and be a fantastic mother to Becca at the same time. I loved spending time with Becca and watching her face every time she experienced something new. Our new home afforded us the space we needed for Becca to grow and for Lauren and I to spend time together decorating and planning for our many years of happiness in this beautiful home.

For Lauren and me, and every other person living in America, life came to an abrupt halt on September 11, 2001. On this day, nineteen Islamic extremists who were part of a terrorist organization called Al-Qaeda attacked our homeland. Those terrorists, led by Osama Bin Laden, hijacked four separate United States commercial airliners and crashed them into the heart of America. The first two hijacked planes were flown into the North and South towers of the World Trade

Center (WTC), the third into the Pentagon, and the fourth and final plane into a field in central Pennsylvania. "9/11," as it forever will be known, was probably the most horrific, catastrophic, and painful day in United States history. It was a wakeup call to all of us who took for granted our peaceful existence. It made everyone realize that there is no longer this imaginary force field that surrounds our great country to protect us from foreign invaders.

On September 10, 2001, I worked my 3 p.m. to 11 p.m. shift at the police department and then participated with my SWAT team on an early morning raid of a suspected drug house. I got home at 7 a.m. on September 11 and quickly fell into a deep sleep. I slept happily, knowing that we had done something good for our community by shutting down a drug operation and by putting the bad guys in jail, at least for a little while.

At 8:46 a.m., I was awoken by a phone call from my best friend, Brian Skelton. He was working the day shift at the police department and he was at the police station watching history unfold before his eyes. I was half asleep when I answered the phone. He told me to turn on the TV because a commercial airliner had just crashed into one of the World Trade Center towers. Not really grasping the gravity of the situation, I told him to leave me alone and not to call me unless he saw a plane flying into MY house!

At 8:50 a.m., I got the first of several more phone calls reporting the same crash. I was now totally awake and I decided that I might as well turn on the TV to see what all the fuss was about. I turned on ABC and saw the first WTC tower engulfed in flames. The reporter, Peter Jennings, a normally calm and reassuring voice during tragedy, sounded panicked. There was confusion as to how this could have occurred. One theory was that it was just a terrible accident.

However, that possibility was soon discounted as false. Reporters began to report on the possibility of a terrorist attack. Now he had my attention! I could not possibly believe that terrorists would have the audacity to attack us on our soil.

We were the invincible U.S.A., the liberators of the oppressed, the high-water mark for all other nations to reach for. Never, I told myself. I could not believe it!

At 9:03 a.m., that possibility became a reality. A second plane was flown into the South Tower of the WTC. I was now feeling extreme sadness for all those people in the buildings, the fire and police personnel who were responding to help, and all those in the streets below who were running for their lives. Every minute—no … every second felt like an eternity. Panic and mayhem was captured on live TV and transmitted around the world. The mighty America was shown to be just as fragile and vulnerable as the rest of the world. We, the largest and most powerful country in the world, were now an unwilling member of a worldwide fraternity whose initiation ritual consists of instilling fear and bloodshed.

At 9:37 a.m., shortly after the second tower was hit, it was reported that terrorists had hijacked another airliner and had flown it into the Pentagon in Washington, D.C., a vicious strike at our nation's capital: the pulse of our government.

At 10:06 a.m., the final wave of terror planned by Osama Bin Laden was quite possibly meant to strike the White House or the U.S. Capitol Building. This attack would have been a success had it not been for some heroic passengers on board the flight that crashed into an open field in Shanksville, Pennsylvania. They were able to bravely fight off the terrorists on board that flight, and without a doubt saved thousands of lives, most notably our elected leaders.

All those images of burning buildings and helpless people jumping out of windows hundreds of feet above the ground, and the knowledge that all these acts were committed by Islamic extremists who spend their lives preaching hate, made it all very personal to me. I had spent the last thirteen years serving my country, helping the oppressed, and fighting the darker side of life. I was trying to control my anger, my HATRED! I wanted to lead the charge into wherever those terrorists came from. I wanted to act and I wanted to do so right then and there.

However, I took a deep breath and I took the time to reflect on how the families of those who lost their lives on that fateful day must have felt. It reminded me of how I felt the day Andy died. The anger, the sorrow, the questions left unanswered. I wondered if those families were feeling that same way. I felt their pain, their desperation, and their sense of hopelessness.

The day after the attacks, I spent a lot of time watching Fox News and CNN, trying to learn more about what had happened and trying to find a way to prevent it from ever happening again. While watching one of the many reports from Washington, D.C., on TV, I decided that it was my duty to find a way to help ensure that 9/11 would never happen again.

I watched as President George Bush talked about reestablishing a once near-defunct counterterrorism agency, one that I cannot actually name due to security reasons. I believed that it was an opportunity for me to do my part for my family, my country, and me.

I went online and printed out the government application form and filled it out. Lauren was dead set against the idea, mostly due to her fear of losing her husband and Becca losing her father. I was able to convince her to at least allow me to apply for the position ... the worst that could happen is that they could offer me a job and I would turn it down. I immediately applied and returned to my normal life as a police officer. I kept the hope of a call offering me a position in the back of my mind, but I did not want to lose sight of my current obligations at the police department.

The rest of 2001 was spent working, planning for future terrorist attacks, and watching the news. However, Lauren and I did have time to discuss adding another member to our family of three. Becca was now approaching five years old and Lauren was getting "baby fever" once again. I was also ready to start trying again, and I was especially hoping to have a son. Selfishly, I wanted a son and I wanted to name him Andrew. However, I knew that neither Lauren nor I had any control over the sex of the baby, and I would be grateful for any healthy child that God provided for us.

In January of 2002, we found out that Lauren was pregnant once again. I couldn't help thinking about the idea of having a son—Andy's namesake, a "mini-me." Lauren kept reminding me that there were no guarantees and that I should not get my hopes up too high. I promised her that I would not allow my heart to be corrupted by the thought of having a son. I knew that she was right and I truly believed that God would make sure that our child, whether it was to be a "he" or a "she," was a healthy and happy baby.

CHAPTER NINETEEN

"Doors"—at least that's what I like to call them—are the opportunities in your life in which you can either choose to pursue or decide to ignore. I am a firm believer in the theory that "doors" open in life for a reason. Each "door" will lead you down a different path or course in life. The decision on whether or not I will enter an open "door" is left up to two distinct criteria: first and foremost, I place my faith in God and I pray for guidance when faced with a decision. The other determining factor is my own conscious evaluation of the opportunity. I always try to ensure that every decision I make has a positive impact on my family, the future, and me.

In March of 2002, I got the call from the United States government, tentatively offering me a position as a counterterrorism agent, pending the results of three days of testing. Lauren was in her third month of the pregnancy, feeling ill, and definitely not happy about the news I had to offer her. I told her that they wanted me to come to their headquarters, located on the East Coast, for three days to go through a battery of physical and psychological tests and to go through an oral interview.

Her initial reaction was, "No way in hell!" I explained to her that I felt in my heart that this was a "door" that I needed to explore further. I did my best to convince her that I had not received any official offer for employment and that I needed to go there to finish the last part of the application process.

I also needed to gather more information about the job. She reluctantly agreed and the following week I was off to explore my possible future employment.

I successfully completed the three days of prodding my mind and body and I performed very well in my oral interview. I was told "informally" that I definitely would be offered a position in the next few weeks. I was able to get answers to all of my questions and I left feeling as if this "door" was definitely worth going through. I returned home and had a long talk with Lauren. We weighed the pros and cons of my current job as a police officer versus the pros and cons of the new position.

After several days of thought, soul searching, and questions, we came to the decision that if offered the job, I should take it. Lauren knew that I was unhappy with the way my current job situation was evolving and she also knew how affected I was by 9/11. I understood her concerns and fears, but I also reminded her that fighting possible terrorists, wherever they might be found, was no more dangerous than being on the SWAT team and going into a building with people shooting at me. Plus, it meant a pay increase and a new challenge that I sorely needed.

A few weeks after I completed my physicals and interview, I got a call from the agency offering me a position as a special agent in the Philadelphia field office. Part of my agreement with Lauren was that we would only agree to the position if we did not have to move from our current home. Luckily, that was not an issue and I accepted the position. I was given a starting date for the academy of May 19, 2002 … about three weeks away!

The academy was in a remote area in the southwestern portion of the United States and it was approximately eight weeks from start to finish. Lauren was happy for me and a little sad for herself when I told her the news, but supportive nonetheless. I spent the next few weeks making sure all possible future problems had a definite solution. I made sure that the grass would be cut, the cars were running well, and that people would help Lauren while I was away. Friends and family were lining up to offer whatever assistance we might need. I also spent those weeks reassuring both Lauren and Becca that I would be home before they knew it and that we were making the right decision.

My reporting date came sooner than I had hoped. I wanted to spend one more day with my family, but that was not going to happen. Lauren and Becca drove me to my pickup point and we said our sad goodbyes. It just about broke my heart to have to kiss them goodbye. Both were crying, as was I, but I knew that this was the right choice. That didn't help my heart at that moment, but as they drove off, I came to realize that my life was changing course once again. I had faith that the decision to go through this particular "door" was the correct one. Par for the course, I asked Andy to keep watch over Lauren and Becca while I was away and I knew in my heart that he would not let me down.

I arrived at the academy and the training was intense. I trained harder than I had ever trained for anything in my life. I met so many great Americans who, like me, wanted to make sure 9/11 never happened again. The instructors, consisting mostly of former U.S. Navy SEALS and the elite U.S. Army Special Forces unit Delta Force, taught us how to fight and defeat all potential terrorist threats. They gave us the ability and the confidence to assure victory. I felt like a superhero. I trained heavily in firearms, knife fighting, close-quarter combat, and ground fighting techniques.

I spoke to Lauren and Becca daily. I wanted to know everything they did each and every day. In early June, Lauren went to the OB/GYN and had her five-month checkup. She also asked her doctor to do an ultrasound test in order to find out the sex of our baby. As I stated earlier, neither of us were too keen on surprises! She had the test and found out the sex of the baby. That night, I called her like I usually did and she told me about the doctor visit. When I asked about the results of the ultrasound, she got very quiet. She sounded disappointed when she told me that we were having a girl. I told her, in a reassuring tone, that I was not upset about the results.

However, just then she got very excited and exclaimed, "I got ya! It's going to be a boy!"

My heart sank and for one of the few times in my life I was speechless! But I soon regained my senses and started to do a little dance, and I shouted as loud as I possibly could, "I'm having a baby boy!" It was meant to be—Andy was meant to live on through my life, and my soon-to-be baby boy would carry his name.

Shortly after hearing the good news about baby Andrew's impending arrival, we were blessed with even more good news—Andy's Court became a reality. I was devastated that I could not be there to witness the unveiling of the building that was created to honor my brother. Thankfully, Lauren, Becca, and my family were there to pay homage to Andy.

One other very important person was sadly absent from the ceremony as well. Andy's mentor, friend, and greatest supporter, Gene Troutman, would not be there to see his greatest masterpiece to completion. He died unexpectedly in the summer of 2001 from a massive heart attack. This had a traumatic effect on my family and made us revisit many of the memories of Andy's time at Innabah. His legacy, along with Andy's, will live on in the building that houses Andy's Court.

As you may recall from earlier in Andy's story, he loved to play basketball. Andy's passion, when not working at the camp, was to challenge other staff members and campers to games of hoops on the old but effective outdoor basketball court. Andy's love for basketball and how he used the sport to bring people together to share in his joy was part of the catalyst for Gene to create the vision for Andy's Court.

Needless to say, Gene's dream and vision came to fruition and he got his wish to incorporate Andy into the building. Andy's Court was open to all who knew him and those who only wished they had. I wrote a poem to honor the building and my brother's legacy. A copy of the poem, along with our pictures, hangs on a wall in the building for all who use the facility to read:

"Andy's Court"

Andy was a special kid;
Thin … about six feet tall.
He wasn't the most gifted athlete
Except when it came to basketball.

Andy was a little awkward at times.
He handled that just fine.
But when it came to "b-ball,"
He always seemed to shine.

Nothing made Andy happier
Than playing a game of hoops.
We'd play one on one for hours.
Andy didn't care whether he'd win or lose.

He had the touch of an angel
When he let go of the ball.
The ball seemed in slow motion
Until through the hoop it would fall.

His fondest days are of Innabah,
Hanging with "Otis" and "Gene."
I've never seen Andy happier
At this place so peaceful and serene.

Now for those that thought he was forgotten,
A distant memory to us all,
Just take a look around you,
At this building so big and tall.

Andy will live in our hearts forever
With his name placed on this wall,
So when you can't find something better to do
Try challenging Andy to a game of "b-ball."

Andy touched so many lives while he was alive. Two people that were instrumental to his success were Kristi and Greg Troutman. Kristi was like a sister to Andy and I, and Greg was like a brother to Andy. Gene Troutman, Greg's father, had raised a beautiful family, and for accepting Andy as one of their own, I am eternally grateful. Greg and Kristi both wanted to write a memory of Andy for the book. As you will see, Andy not only gave love but received it as well:

"About Andy" by Greg Troutman

I remember Andy not for one specific incident but I remember him for what he taught me about life. Andy, even though he was slow cognitively, was advanced psychologically. Andy taught me to enjoy every moment of life and to look on the bright side in every situation. I remember him as always smiling. Camp Innabah was like a safe haven for Andy. He was one of the gang. We all laughed with him and didn't judge him for his differences. I, personally, found it easy to like Andy for Andy. It was that simple. I could always count on him for a game of basketball or for making me laugh.

When I look back on him now, I realize even more how much he understood life. Andy believed in God and always enjoyed himself. He could be cutting grass the entire day in extreme heat and he'd still have a smile on his face when he gave you a thumbs-up. Andy felt lucky to be at Innabah. I know my father, Gene, counted Andy as another son. I remember him telling me how great Andy's attitude was and how he was such a hard worker. There was no slacking in Andy. Gene worked hard, until his own death, in creating Andy's Court for the camp. Andy's Court is a gymnasium for the campers to enjoy sports like he did.

Andy had such an impact on my wife, Kristi, and my life that we named our firstborn son Derek Andrew. His middle name is after Andy. We are all proud to have known him, and miss his smile and thumbs-up attitude.

Kristi's input came in the form of a letter to Andy. She had told me how difficult it was for her to put her feelings and emotions into words. She did not want to sound "stupid" and did not want to lessen the impact of Andy's story with a "lame" contribution. I assured her that neither Andy nor I could ever think those things about her and I encouraged her to write from the heart and to let the words flow from her heart to the page. I was brought to tears when I read her letter to Andy. It was perfect and I could not have asked for a better contribution to Andy's story than the one she provided:

Dear Andy,

I think the best way to convey my thoughts is to write you a letter. I pray you are in a place where you can feel my words of gratitude, for you taught me so much. When I think about our friendship, the memories clearly present themselves in two parts. In childhood, you were "Cousin Andy" and truly my best friend. The memories and moments we shared were numerous and priceless. I remember mud pies on the patio and leaf piles in the back yard. We had fun just jumping in from ground level. We left flying in from the picnic bench and the other contraptions to the daredevils, Billy and Matt. I know we got stuck with the "re-rake the leaves" job more, but I didn't care, did you? Thanks for always being there to play. I don't ever remember arguing or fighting with you over the rules of the games or the outcomes. You were always a good sport. You know how much I could go on with the stories of what we did together but it is, after all, Matt's book, so I'll try to limit myself. He always was the "storyteller" and I'm proud he is putting his skill to good use.

This memoir would not be complete without the highlights from Rehoboth Beach. This annual trip was something we could all count on. Our moms made sure of it. Where do I start? The look-alike outfits or the "who belongs to who" game? You think it would get old, but as much as we said "not again," we secretly liked the pairings. Do you agree, "Brother Andy"? Now for the infamous and somewhat tragic tandem-bike ride! Okay, we kissed the sand pretty hard but boardwalks aren't really that wide anyway! At least we tried. This leads me to ask, "Can you believe your mother rides on a two-wheel motorcycle when we could not get her off the three-wheel bicycle in all those years?" I really enjoyed running from the waves and building sandcastles. It was always nice to have a friend who agreed that going deeper than knee high was scary!

Andy, what I want you to know is that you were my best friend. When we were young, I didn't even think about the fact that you had to struggle more than others did. Yes, you stuttered ... but I was painfully timid. That is just who we were. I know that I could often finish your sentences if I wanted, but I tried not to. I am thankful that the innocence of childhood allowed us the opportunity to be such good friends without being clouded by life's struggles. We were very much alike in our interests and fears.

The next group of memories comes later during our late-teenage and early adulthood years. As I grew up I became more aware of how difficult things could be for you and how ugly the world could be sometimes. We didn't have as frequent contact, as often happens as we grow and life's business takes over. I want you to know that you were always in my thoughts, and I believe God knew that too. I suppose that is why I was led toward Greg and Camp Innabah. I never thought you needed help, just an opportunity to shine. I remember listening to Gene, my future father-in-law, as he talked about the need for help at the camp. Here was an opportunity to come into an open, friendly, and Christian environment. I was so happy when you started to volunteer at the camp. Like I said, you needed an opportunity to shine and shine you did. You moved from volunteer to paid employee and Gene would thank me for sending you his way. I think the greatest thing was hearing other staff/teens talk about you when I would see them at the house. They did not know of our lifelong connection and I was not involved with the camp, so their words were from the heart. There was always something positive being said about you. Your hard work and dedication inspired many of the staff.

I remember coming into the Troutmans' house and you were lying on the floor watching television. It was as if things had come full circle again; my friend hanging out with me again. Andy, I remember your smile and the stories I was told from the basketball court. You know, Greg was a little late for a few dates because he was shooting hoops with you. Your presence around the Innabah/Troutman house helped me know that this was the type of family I wanted to become a part of because they saw you for you and not for any disabilities. Thank you for that.

As I've said, the memories would fill a book, and Matt is surely covering that. I feel comfort in knowing you left this world when you were on top. It was much too soon in this mortal's eyes, but your impact on my life was immeasurable. Thank you and I love you.

Love,
Kristi

Andy's Court was now a place to learn, to grow, and to share. Those were all the things that Andy did while at Camp Innabah. It would never have come to fruition had it not been for Gene, his family, and all of the financial contributions and prayers from so many people who knew and loved my brother. I struggled with the guilt of not being there to witness the unveiling, but I also knew that my training would be over soon and I would be able to see it when I got home.

Finally, the eight long weeks of intense training had finally come to an end and I arrived very late at night at Philadelphia International Airport. On the other side of the security checkpoint was my extremely pregnant but radiantly beautiful wife! As I exited the terminal and saw her for the first time in two months, I felt that familiar feeling inside, the same one I had on the day we married … intense, life-altering admiration and love! I had missed her so much. I embraced her, held her tight, and whispered into her ear that I never wanted to let her go. She replied, "You better not!" I was home and ready to take a few days off to be with my family. I couldn't wait to see Becca in the morning. I couldn't wait to see how much she had grown and hold her in my arms. There is definitely no place like home!

The "Best Men." *Left to right:* Chris Gilroy, Brian Skelton, Lauren, Matt, Kevin Gilroy, and Jamie Hall Jr.

Matt and Lauren.

Left to right: Kristi, Greg, Derek Andrew, and Kalina Troutman.

Exterior view of "Andy's Court" on the grand opening of this marvelous tribute to my brother, Andy Cubbler. June 2002.

CHAPTER TWENTY

I completed my training with flying colors. I came home feeling like I was on top of the world. I started working immediately, feeling like I had a new purpose in life, one of monumental importance. The world was still feeling the effects of 9/11 and they needed to know that they could live once again in safety. It was my job to ensure that a day like 9/11 would never, ever happen again. Not on my watch and, by the grace of God, not on anyone else's watch either!

As the summer came to a close, Lauren was more than ready to have the baby. She was hot, tired, and uncomfortable. Unfortunately for her, she still had another month or so till her due date. The only thing that was keeping her from losing her mind was the peaceful knowledge that came with not having to get her classroom prepared for the upcoming school year. That week before school started was usually a nightmare for Lauren. She would spend hours putting up posters, bulletin boards, and getting her lesson plans together.

This year, however, there would be none of that! She was set to begin her one-year maternity leave and was looking forward to spending those first months with our new baby boy. We both felt that this was the right thing for her to do, especially since my new job afforded us a little more financial stability.

Baby Andrew was soon to arrive, and the anticipation was killing us! As her due date drew nearer, I was feeling a lot of anxiety about constantly being away from home, due to the constraints of my new job, and possibly missing the birth of our child! Since Becca had been five weeks early when she was born, my fear was that Andrew would come early and I would not be there to see his birth. I had planned to take some time off to help out Lauren with baby Andrew and to watch over Becca. I was just concerned that I did not take off early enough. Thankfully, Lauren did not go into labor until my time off from work had begun.

Early in the evening on September 19, 2002, Lauren complained of what she thought were labor pains. We decided to go to the hospital, just in case. Labor with Becca stretched over two days and Lauren was prepared to go the distance once again. We arrived at the hospital, but after an exam by her doctor, we were sent home. She was definitely having contractions, but the doctor felt she was not dilated enough to be admitted. Lauren was a little disappointed; she was definitely ready to have the baby. We came back home and went straight to bed for a good night of sleep, or so we thought!

At 12 a.m. on September 20, just a few hours after the doctor sent us home, Lauren's water broke. She tried in vain to wake me up. Unfortunately, I was in one of those deep slumbers and I did not respond to her attempts. Finally, she had to vigorously shake me and she loudly told me that "it was time"!

Once I heard those magic words, the ones that all impending fathers have stamped into their minds—"It's time"—I popped right out of bed and took control of the situation. Lauren was very calm; I wish I could have said the same for me! Still half asleep and trying to go over the mental checklist in my head, I was going a little crazy. She calmed me down enough to let me know that her water had just broken and that we needed to go to the hospital. Luckily, I still had all the bags packed from our earlier visit, so we set our sights for the hospital.

As we drove, I kept one eye on my beautiful wife and one on the road. She was having contractions but was handling them rather well. She assured me that she was fine and that I needed to concentrate on getting us there safely! We arrived and this time the doctor admitted Lauren into the maternity ward. Great ... first hurdle complete! Now all we needed was pain medicine for Lauren and eventually a baby. Piece of cake, I thought ... yeah, right!

Lauren's contractions were fast and painful now that we were at the hospital. She wanted an epidural and she wanted it fast! The anesthesiologist was summoned and he arrived within minutes. He prepared the epidural and advised Lauren that she needed to be perfectly still, since he was sticking a gigantic needle into her spine! I was never one for needles and I certainly did not like watching some stranger stick one into my wife's spine!

On the first attempt, he missed his mark and had to pull it back out. After the failed second attempt, he blamed Lauren for moving. He actually scolded her for doing so, but Lauren was not moving; in fact, she was so scared that she was almost a statue! Lauren was now in pain from the labor and the gigantic needle being stuck in and pulled out of her back. She had also begun to cry. This made me a little upset as well.

So, prior to his third attempt at administering the epidural, I whispered into the anesthesiologist's ear, "For your sake, you better make it this time!" He looked at me with a little bit of annoyance and a whole lot of fear. Not that I wanted to add any more pressure on him, but I was ready to stick that needle in HIS spine for hurting my wife! Luckily for him, he got it right on that third attempt.

Lauren, feeling better knowing that the medicine would begin to take effect soon, closed her eyes and tried to get a little sleep. She was expecting another long labor, just like we had with Becca; however, that was not to be. Andrew must have been really ready to join the world, because at 4:35 a.m., Andrew was born! Lauren's epidural had not even had a chance to totally take hold before she began pushing. Before we knew it, the doctor was handing her our beautiful son, Andrew Lucas Cubbler! He was magnificent! Andrew weighed in at a hefty eight pounds five ounces and was twenty and a half inches long.

God had answered our prayers by creating the most beautiful and angelic baby boy that the world had ever seen. As I held him in my arms for the first time and looked into the big, blue eyes of my beautiful newborn son, I saw something very comforting, almost familiar. What I saw that day was my brother, Andy, looking back at me and I smiled. It was as if he were right there, sharing in all the joy and excitement, the way I had wished it would be all along!

We were now a family of four, Lauren, Becca, Andrew, and I. Becca was now a doting "big sister" and loving every moment with her knew little brother. Lauren was more at ease with Andrew, having learned the ropes with Becca. Shortly after we brought Andrew home, we had family and friends over to the house. Nan, Pop, Mom and Paul, and several friends of the family were over to meet the newest member of the Cubbler family.

Unbeknownst to anyone in the room, Nan had a surprise gift that can only be described as a gift from heaven. She had a large, rectangular box, neatly wrapped in a baby motif. She handed the box to me, which I initially thought was strange. Usually the mother gets to open all the gifts when a new baby is celebrated.

I carefully opened the box, since Nan spends meticulous amounts of time wrapping them. Once the paper was removed and folded neatly for Lauren to possibly reuse at a later date, I opened the box. Inside the box was a hand-made quilt. It was full of yellow, red, and blue swatches of cloth, and in the center was a brown teddy bear with the name "Andy" underneath of the bear.

At first, I did not grasp the significance of the quilt. Granted it was beautiful, but I am a guy and quilts just don't do it for me! However, Nan told to take a closer look at the quilt. As I studied the fabric, the colors, and the stitched name "Andy," it dawned on me. The quilt was made out of my brother's clothes!

The week before Andy's death, he was spending nights at Nan and Pop's house. Andy was working maintenance at the Frederick Mennonite Home and he wore a uniform of blue pants and a brown shirt with "Andy" stitched over the left breast pocket. Nan was doing all of his laundry that week, and as it turns out, she never was able to let go of his clothes after he died. No one new that for the past thirteen years she had kept all of his clothes, let alone that she had them neatly stored in the attic for what turned out to be this particular and very special day. His red and blue bandanas, a yellow button-down shirt, and his brown work shirt were all used to make the quilt for baby Andrew.

I usually do not cry in public, especially around my mom. Crying is contagious and when my mom gets going, there is no stopping the tears from streaming down her face. I held back the tears, more out of fear of showing the pain of Andy's death still inside my soul, but the lump in my throat was immense. Mom, Lauren, and everyone else was either crying or trying not to cry. I believe that Nan held on to Andy's clothes for a reason. I believe that she was meant to keep those clothes for a very specific purpose: the birth of baby Andrew.

I do not believe in coincidences. I believe that everything in life happens for a particular reason. This gesture of love meant more to me than words could possibly describe. It was the tangible piece of my brother that I needed to help me heal. Nothing in this world will ever replace my brother and no person will ever be as special as he was to me.

However, in that room, in my home, there were so many people who loved both Andy and me. On that day, I felt all their love and energy and it made me stronger. It made me realize the love that I had found in Lauren and the joy I had in watching my children grow. I found perspective. I found meaning. I found myself, once lost and without focus.

I knew what I was meant to be … a good son, a good grandson, a good husband and father, a good public servant, a good friend and most of all, a good brother. Nothing more and nothing less. Everything else was just icing on the cake! If I could accomplish being "good" at all those things, my life would be a success. At the age of thirty-two, I had finally found out who I was and why I was placed on this Earth to begin with. What a relief!

FINAL CHAPTER

Shortly after receiving the quilt from Nan, I did what I fondly call my "self-check." Up until this time, I was known to keep a grudge against anyone who wronged my family or me. I believed that until things were made right, that individual would be kept on my "list" of people I could not forgive. I decided that part of being a "good" person was being able to let go of my grudges and to make peace with those who offended me. I began to make a list of all of the people who, in some shape or form, wronged my family or me. At the top of that list was my father.

I had not spoken to him in close to seven years and had no idea where he was living or if he was even still alive. Thanks to modern technology, namely the Internet, I found that my father was living down South. He had retired from teaching in Pennsylvania and had moved there to live out his retirement. However, he was now teaching at a Christian school and I found his name and address listed on the Internet.

I sat down at the computer and wrote him a letter. The following is an excerpt from that letter to my father:

Dad,

I am sure that you are not only shocked to hear from me but also probably a little upset. The reason I am writing to you is due to my desire to "bury the hatchet." I've spent the last year reflecting on my life and what has become of it, and

I felt that one of the most important things I needed to do was to learn how to forgive and let go of my grudges. I began to write a book about Andy, and through this book, there has come a sort of healing, and understanding of what my life has been and what I want it to be from now on. I realized that even though Andy and I spent a large portion of our childhood trying to win your heart, I cannot spend my adult life hating you for not being able to give it to me.

As you know, I married Lauren and shortly after the wedding, we became pregnant. Our daughter, Rebecca Linne, is now six and a half and a smart, beautiful, and loving child. She starts first grade on Tuesday and I am amazed how grown up she has become already. I also have a son, Andrew Lucas, who will be two years old on September 20. He is the spitting image of me as a child, and according to Mom, just as stubborn as I was as well.

I had a change in careers as well. I left the police department in 2002 and was hired as a counterterrorism agent in the U.S. government, as a result of the 9/11 attacks. It has been over two years now since I made the switch and I am looking forward to the future and what it holds in my career.

Another reason for my writing you is to once and for good tell you that I have forgiven you for all the things I feel you did and did not do for me and Andy as children growing up. I am not sure if you even care about my forgiveness or if you even feel I have the right to forgive you for things you may not feel you have done, but I am offering it anyway.

I know you are teaching again at this school and I am sure you are living the life you want with Janet and Katherine. I do not wish to have a relationship with you or Janet, but at some time I would like to have one with Katherine, if she wants to. I know she may not remember much about me and she may not want to know me, but I do love her and would like to someday be able to explain my side of the story to her.

Beginning a new relationship with you would only make my life more complicated. I have two beautiful kids and they only know one set of grandparents. I do not want to confuse them or cause them any sadness by telling them that they have another grandfather to deal with. I just think that would not be fair to them, Lauren, Mom and Paul, or me, for that matter.

I just wanted you know that I forgive you, occasionally think about you, and most of all, I want you to live the life you have now and know that you no longer need to worry about my life or me and how it may or may not be working out. I will be just fine and I have come to grips with my past and am only looking forward to the future for my family and me. If this letter seemed a little arrogant or presumptuous, I apologize. I did not know if you needed to hear any of this or not, but I needed to say it. Thanks for reading it and take care!

I mailed the letter to the address I found on the Internet, omitting my return address. Outwardly, I presented the appearance that I was satisfied with sending the letter with no chance for a retort from Dad. However, in some strange way, I actually had hoped that he would take the time to respond. That would mean that he had thought enough about the letter, good or bad, to look me up, sit down, and write a response. That, in some way, would validate my desire for all of those years to win his approval.

That apparently was not meant to be. I never received a response and I have no idea if he ever received the letter to begin with. I do have the peace of mind of knowing that I was able to put down thirty-three years of frustration and pain on paper and send it to my father. I forgave him and I hope he spends the rest of his days with the knowledge that I hold no grudges against him.

My only wish for the future, as far as my father is concerned, is to someday see my sister, Katherine, once again. I want her to know that I still love her and never wanted to be apart from her. She will be eighteen years old soon and old enough to know the reasons for the ending of the relationship between our father and me. I am not sure if she will even remember me, but it is definitely something I can hope to accomplish before it is too late.

I continued to go down my mental "grudge list" and made every effort to reach out to each and every person who had in one way or another wronged my family or me. For the most part, I was able to make contact with those individuals, and I took the time to explain why I was initiating the contact and why it was so important for me to forgive them. Some seemed oblivious to the fact that they had even done anything wrong. Some intimated that they had wanted to call or stop by to apologize for whatever might have caused the strain on our personal relationship. A few did not care if I forgave them and had no interest in my attempts to make things right. No matter what the outcome was, I was once again at peace with my efforts to clean the slate of my extensive "grudge list."

This book was my therapy, and I needed to write all of these emotions and feelings down so I could tell the story of my amazing brother's life. Throughout the book, I have personal memories of those who knew and loved Andy. This book would not be complete without the memories of our grandmother Nan. I wanted to capture her emotions, her memories, and the impact he had on her life. Andy was her "special friend," and when he died, she felt his pain, his struggles, and his love. It took everything she had inside of her to relive those painful memories, organize her thoughts, and somehow put those emotions onto paper.

Somehow, Nan was also able to incorporate the tragedy of 9/11 into her piece, without knowing that I would write about that day in the book. The words, the anger, and the love of a grandmother grieving, still today for her lost grandson, can be felt in the following passage:

Last year [2004] in recognition of 9/11, the parents and grandparents of those lost were acknowledged, thus acknowledging that grandparents also grieve. The hurt of Andy's death and the feeling of "If I could just get to him—I could make him undead" are burned in my brain forever. The sadness of wanting the whole world to stop, because Andy was dead, seemed too heavy to bear.

Instead people went to work, watched TV, bought new clothes, and even LAUGHED. Andy was dead and people talked in loud voices and laughed! Andy would have been more respectful. The good times are just as real—the visits, the meals, the new clothes, birthday cakes, soccer games, baseball facts, church services, camp visits, graduation, and the cards for my "special friend."

Andy taught me (and I never got an A in this course) how to forgive. His life was full of total forgiveness. He was never suspicious, greedy, or distrustful. I still use him as a yardstick when I don't know which way to go. What would Andy do?

One of my greatest joys was last year when my grandson, Daniel, my daughter's son, came home from a week at Camp Innabah. He talked about how much everyone used Andy's Court. I know Andy is proud to have his name on a building at Innabah, and he's there making sure EVERYONE is included.

Although Andy Cubbler's life ended so tragically that fateful afternoon on July 12, 1989, at the age of twenty-one, the magnitude of the life he led and the lives he touched are still being revealed to this day. You see, not only was Andy my brother, he was my guardian angel. I am convinced that God placed him on this Earth to show me and the rest of world that life is not about good looks, fancy cars, making lots of money, or even being able to say a complete sentence without stuttering! Andy's message was simple: Show love for all people, walk in the path that God has made for you, and have the strength and courage to conquer your fears.

It has been sixteen years since he has been gone, at least physically. My course in life has taken many turns and there have been several "doors" that have been opened for me to explore. Looking back on my life with Andy and my life after his death, I can see how each and every "door" that has opened for me had his hand print somewhere on the door knob. I am convinced that had it not been for Andy's life and his influence on me after his death, I would never have accomplished everything that I have in life.

My family is now complete. Baby Andrew is now well into his toddler years. He is walking, playing, smiling, and talking. He is a joy to behold and is well on his way to making his uncle Andy and me very proud. Becca is turning into a smart, beautiful, and respectful young lady who is so interested to learn about her uncle Andy. Lauren is as beautiful today as she was the night we met and I fell in love with her. I measure each day against the last, hoping only that Andy would approve of how I did that particular day.

Andy's memory and his legacy live on each and every day in the lives of so many people. Each person who knew Andy does at times look back on what he meant to him or her. Whether it is in times of trouble or in times when things are going so great that they have to thank someone for helping them get to that point, the person they go to is Andy. There was just something about him that drew all these people to him. It was his spirit, his joy of life, and his unwavering optimism that everything is going to be all right.

If there is one thing I want my son and daughter to know about their uncle Andy, it is that he would have loved them very much. He would have loved to have seen them grow and he would have loved to have steered them through all the good and hard times that life has in store for them both. He would have been their "cool" uncle Andy. He would have been their biggest supporter. He would have attended every one of Rebecca's gymnastics classes and he would have been the one to teach little Andrew the art of the perfect jump shot.

Unfortunately for those who loved him so much, he won't be here to share in all those amazing experiences. God had called him home. His job on Earth was done, at least in a physical sense. I can only hope and pray that I do not let him down. I have to be the one to teach Andrew how to shoot a perfect jump shot. I have to make sure I attend all of Rebecca's gymnastic classes and I have to be the one to ensure that they learn about life and all that it entails. Most of all, I have to be the one who loves them so much that Andy can feel it in the heavens.

One thing I am sure of is that Andy is watching over all of us, protecting us every day, just as I had tried to protect him for all the years he graced us with his life here on Earth.

As my children continue to grow, learn, and experience life through untainted eyes, I hope that this book and the memories it contains can help them "know" the Uncle Andy they never had the pleasure to meet. I hope it can serve as a guide for them to read if they are lost and confused, happy or sad, or if they feel they need to reach out to Andy and look to his life story for wisdom.

Most of all, I wanted to ensure that the world knew of Andy. He never felt like he belonged in this world. This is my way of making sure that he knows that not only did he belong in this world, he also made a difference in it as well. His memory will not be forgotten. His story will live on in the pages of this book and in the hearts of all those who loved him so dearly.

The End

AFTERWORD

A Parent's Thoughts

By

Rev. Paul L. Jones
&
Louise Linnemeier (Cubbler) Jones

A Mother's Thoughts

What do you do with a broken heart? When Andy died in 1989, my heart broke. Determined to "stand tall" under the pain of his death and of Matthew's departure for military service in Germany, I went back into my high school classroom. As fate would have it, the book I taught that fall was John Gunther's memoir of his young son's death, *Death Be Not Proud*. Facing the pain in that book, along with the insights and wisdom and listening ears of my students, I began to put my life together—or so I thought.

Like so many children of the '60s, I had come out of high school and college filled with the mantra, "Ask not what your country can do for you; ask what you can do for your country." I was always determined to try to make the world a better place—at least in my corner of it. I know after Andy's death, I became a better teacher....I had Andy's "story" to share with my students, and for those who struggled Andy's story became a beacon of hope.

I was equally determined to be the best mom I knew how to be. Ever since they were born, I never let a day go by without telling Matt and Andy I loved them. Loving them was as basic as "breathing." With only Matt left, that need to show him he was loved increased many-fold.

Seven years would pass. I could honestly say my faith, my beloved husband, and my vocation, friends, and family carried me all that time. Matt was home safe from Desert Storm and working as a police officer. I was proud and happy. Then breast cancer struck.

The course of chemotherapy and radiation would defeat that enemy. Unbeknownst to me, another even more deadly demon would surface: heart failure. In February of 2002, I went to school unable to breathe and left early to get an echocardiogram that my doctor had ordered—just in case it wasn't asthma but my heart.

I was diagnosed with cardio-myopathy. My heart muscle had been damaged by one of the chemotherapy drugs and my ejection fraction was a mere 10 percent … the prognosis was grim.

I began a spiritual journey surrounded by a great cloud of witnesses who prayed ceaselessly for me. I worked with a spiritual advisor and discovered I had one big problem. I could not talk to God about myself. I could pray for world hunger, for the homeless, for the needy, for the sick person in my midst, for my husband, children, and grandchildren, but not for myself.

One day, I took my dilemma to my granddaughter, Rebecca. In true Rebecca fashion, she offered to help me pray. She got down on her knees by my bedside and she asked what I wanted to say. I thought that maybe we should tell God my heart was sick. She said, "No, Nana, let's tell him your heart is broken."

"What then?" I wondered.

"Nana! Just tell God to fix it!"

So we did.

The past two years have been filled with that prayer and with rest … eighteen months of essentially being in a recliner. I also had remarkable medical care and I am now working with a 25-percent ejection fraction…. Healing has begun.

Matt's willingness to "go where it hurts" and write this memoir of his brother has also opened the flood gates to all the places I have hurt as well. I have realized that by "standing up" under the greatest grief of my life, I also have bottled it up. The pressure that built up continued to break an already broken heart…. Now, seventeen years of pressure are finally being "let go."

God has promised healing to his people. I don't know that I will ever have a physically healed heart, but I do know that my broken heart is being "fixed" and I have my son, Matthew, to thank for a great part of that healing.

Hurts have to be "released;" Andy's spirit has to be "released" as well. Matt's love has to be "released." May the words of this book help others face their hurts, release them, and find the peace that comes from an abiding love that never ends.

I have realized this profound truth about my life. I did not have to "stand tall" … but the love inside me and the love Andy epitomized do. The love we share as a family does.

What do you do with a broken heart? Share your story. Love as you have been loved. Know that God does heal. Celebrate the gift of your children's lives.

May you be as richly blessed by my son's book as I have been.

Louise Linnemeier (Cubbler) Jones

A "Dad's" Thoughts

As Mom and I reared you and Andy, we really had one goal in mind: that we would be able to offer you a firm foundation upon which you could build your lives. We aimed to give you love, direction, values, faith, and a perspective on life that would enable you to endure any hardship, enjoy each celebration, and share your heart with someone special.

A Brother's Love is tangible proof that you truly understand what is really important in life. The book not only tells the moving story of Andy, but the book tells the beautiful story of you and the ways in which you have been transformed by the grace of God and the example of your brother.

By writing this memoir, you have done something that most people, including myself, could never do. You have opened your heart to the whole world. You have revealed your innermost thoughts and feelings. You have risked putting yourself out there for all to see.

And I am so proud of you for loving that much! Your words have already prompted healing among those who have known Andy. Your words are nudging people like me to find light in the midst of darkness. Your words will continue to be instruments of forgiveness and hope for everyone who turns a page of *A Brother's Love*. I am unable to find the words of gratitude to adequately express my appreciation to you for the healing that has come through this book and from your heart.

As you recollect in the book, a memorable photo was taken at the time of Andy's seventeenth birthday party. The photo pictured Andy and his boss/mentor, Gene Troutman, posing with broad smiles and with their trademark "thumbs-up." At various times in *A Brother's Love*, you wondered what Andy would think of your husbanding, fathering, and overall living.

Please know, dear son, Andy gives you "both thumbs-up!" Throughout the book, that image of him came to my mind's eye. I picture him saying to you, "Way to go, Bro!"

With love and pride, I can only join Andy and give you an enthusiastic "thumbs-up." I say, "Way to go, Matt," not only on this book, but also on your family, your perspective, your life, and the way you uplift what really matters most. It is my humble privilege and greatest joy to be part of your journey.

Thank you for sharing your heart with me. Thank you for being the excellent husband and fine father that you are. Thank you for being the best son a man could ever desire. Thank you for calling me "Dad."

Rev. Paul L. Jones

About the Author

As a tribute to my beloved brother, Andy Cubbler, I wrote *A Brother's Love: A Memoir*. I was born and raised in Pottstown, Pennsylvania, located in suburban Philadelphia. Upon graduation from high school, I served for four years in the U.S. Army as an intelligence analyst. I am also a Gulf War veteran. My unit's tour in the Gulf War was chronicled in the book *Silently We Defend*, written by an old army buddy, Robert Benfer, in 2003.

From 1994 to 2002, I served as a police officer in suburban Philadelphia. I was a member of the SWAT team, serving as an assistant team leader, SWAT instructor, and firearms instructor.

After the tragedy of 9/11, I felt compelled to join the fight against terror. In early 2002, I was hired as a special agent with the U.S. government, serving as a counterterrorism specialist. I continue to serve in this capacity to this day.

In 1997, I married the love of my life, Lauren. We now have two beautiful children, Rebecca Linne, who is seven years old, and Andrew Lucas, who is three years old. Without their constant love, support, and encouragement, *A Brother's Love: A Memoir* would never have been written.

Louise and Paul Jones, my mother and stepfather, continue to be a source of strength and love. Not only did my mother raise Andy and me to be the men she hoped we would be, she also served as my editor for the book. Louise is a retired high school English teacher who was instrumental in the historical correctness of the content in the book. Paul is a minister in the United Church of Christ and a constant reminder of the man I hope to become.

CPSIA information can be obtained
at www.ICGtesting.com
Printed in the USA
BVHW080719050319
541761BV00001B/2/P